WALKS IN HIGH HILLS COUNTRY

Northumberland
NATIONAL PARK

Produced and published by Northumberland
County Council National Park Division,
Eastburn, South Park, Hexham, Northumberland
NE46 1BS.

The National Park gratefully acknowledges the
Northumberland Estates, the Lilburn Estates,
the College Valley Estates, the Allgood Estates,
the Ministry of Defence, Forest Enterprise and all
landowners and farmers who agreed to walks on
their land. The routes were chosen by National
Park Rangers and field staff carried out stiling
and waymarking.

Text by Beryl Charlton
Introduction by Tony Hopkins
Designed and illustrated by Eric Dale
Maps by Ann Rooke
Photography by Ken Baker, Jeffrey Beazley,
Eric Dale, Jimmy Givens, Allan Potts,
John D. Wilson and National Park Staff.
Artwork and Origination by The Design Quarter,
Jesmond, Newcastle upon Tyne.
Printed by Smith Print Group, Gateshead,
Tyne and Wear.
The picture on page 17 is reproduced by kind
permission of Barry Nicholson.

The plans on pages 26 and 55 were drawn by
Professor G. Jobey and are reproduced by kind
permission of the Society of Antiquaries,
Newcastle upon Tyne.

With the exception of Walks 11, 14 and 18 the
maps are to a scale of 3 inches to one mile and
are reproduced from the Ordnance Survey
1:25,000 Maps with the permission of the
Controller of Her Majesty's Stationery Office.
© Crown Copyright.

ISBN O 907632 31 9

WALKS
in High Hills
Country

A guide to eighteen walks of between 6.5km (4 miles)
and 14.5km (9 miles) in the Cheviot Hills,
Upper Coquetdale and Simonside

Northumberland
NATIONAL PARK

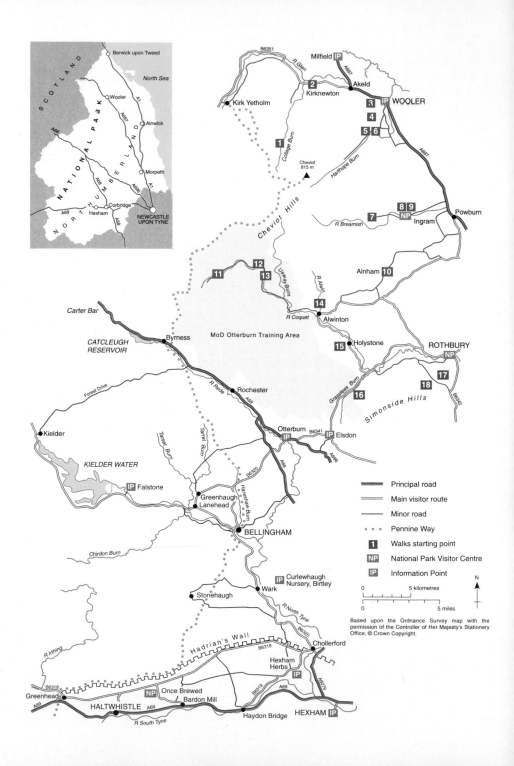

Contents

ENGLAND is a compact and congested country and it comes as a surprise to discover on its northern border an elemental landscape of wide horizons and lonely settlements.

Some of the most challenging walking country in Britain is to be found within Northumberland National Park; the Pennine Way, Hadrian's Wall and a host of old drove roads and ridge paths, famous or forgotten, lattice the hills and valleys. For people who enjoy getting out into the countryside but appreciate accurate guidance and along-the-way information, this book gathers together some of the best and most interesting shorter walks in the northern half of the National Park, from the Border ridge and Cheviot valleys to the Simonside Hills.

THE NATIONAL PARKS of England and Wales are unique in that they do not enshrine or preserve natural landscapes: they were created from farmed and managed land with a long history of settlement, unlike the 'Wilderness' Parks of the United States or the Game Parks of Africa. Britain's Parks are not state owned. The character or flavour of the countryside is so interwoven with traditional farming that it is hard to imagine what it would have looked like if it had not felt the cut of the plough or the footfall of a million sheep.

So, the 'wide blue yonder' of the National Park is not really wilderness at all and access should never be taken for granted. Rules of trespass apply as they do on any other private land, growing crops are easily damaged and the Ministry of Defence live firing ranges are closed to public access for most of the year. But in addition to its conservation aims the National Park has a duty to encourage the provision of facilities for visitors. Footpaths are signposted, car parks and picnic sites maintained, access agreements are negotiated, and there are Visitor Centres and other outlets providing advice and information. This book is an example of team work within the National Park, dealing with interpretation, conservation and rights of way and with the farming community, landowners and visitors.

National Parks were established in the 1950s to conserve and enhance the natural beauty of outstanding upland areas of England and Wales amounting to one tenth of the land surface. Northumberland was the ninth to be designated, in 1956. The National Park Authority acts as a safeguard, a planning authority and an influence on agricultural and forestry developments. Within the Park farmers raise sheep and cattle, foresters crop timber, soldiers fight mock battles – and conservation officers and Rangers talk to landowners, devise management agreements and try to keep the landscape alive and healthy. Within the National Park there are many Sites of Special Scientific Interest, two National Nature Reserves and a host of local Nature Reserves. Thus within a wide framework of landscape protection, the Park Authority encourages conservation whilst taking into account the essential economic and social roles of agriculture, forestry and military training in the future of Northumberland.

The hills and valleys of the Cheviot Hills, and the outlying sandstone ridges, are farmed traditionally for suckler cattle and sheep; every hilltop has its heft of blackface or Swaledale sheep, and every valley has its flocks of Cheviot sheep and herds of Continental-cross cattle. In every nook and cranny there are flowers and ferns, and every sweep of heather has its curlews and pipits, with a visiting sparrowhawk or merlin to add a touch of excitement. Most of the walks in this book start and end in the main Cheviot valleys, the Breamish (3) and Harthope (2), College (2) and Coquet (5). Several are over Ministry of Defence land, part of the Otterburn Training Area's non-firing zone and perfectly safe to walk. Three are on Simonside, with views over Coquetdale to the Cheviot massif. All the walks offer an insight into the unique character of the high hills, the heart of the National Park.

NORTHUMBERLAND NATIONAL PARK covers 1030 square kilometres (398 square miles); it comprises Hadrian's Wall, Tynedale and Wark Forest – places covered in the publication 'Walks in Reiver Country' – as well as the great sweep of high hills embracing the Cheviot massif and the Simonside ridge included in this collection of National Park walks.

The northern part of the National Park is dominated by the Cheviots; there is a unity and coherence about this landscape, allowing each walk to be a variation on a theme. Most of the British countryside has evolved through piecemeal development, setting a few acres of woodland beside a farmstead and a factory beside a river bank. Centuries of this kind of settlement, together with a temperate climate, some complex geology and a big population means we live in a cluttered and crowded land. A walk on open hills, without a living soul for miles around, makes a profound impression.

The story of the Cheviots began about 380 million years ago with a series of volcanic explosions. Ash and lava spread out to cover an area of 906 square kilometres (350 square miles), and when the lava cooled it formed a pink/purple rock called andesite. Soon after the volcanic extrusion came an intrusion; magma was pushed up below the surface and cooled slowly to form granite. Where the hot granite touched the existing andesite it hardened it, and when the andesite massif was weathered and worn away by water and ice the more resistant granite core, and the 'aureole' of hardened tors, were exposed. Today most of the weathered granite lies below a cap of peat on the summits of Cheviot and Hedgehope, whilst the tors are craggy pimples on the broad domes of outlying hills. Because andesite is basic in composition the soil is covered with grass rather than with heather; only on the highest ground, on Cheviot and on the ridge crests where peat has formed to blot out the base soil, does heather grow at all well.

For millions of years the Cheviot massif was an island in a shallow sea, but then a great river developed which dumped a thick bed of sand around the foothills. The Harbottle and Simonside hills, and the terraces of Rothbury, are the remains of this 1,000 foot layer of sandstone, set out in a broad arc with a steep scar slope facing the Cheviots to the north and west.

Weathering and advances by icecaps and glaciers, finally rounded off the contours of the hills and valleys, creating the familiar profile we see today. The earliest signs of human settlement in the Northumberland hills date back about 5,000 years and for most of the intervening period the Cheviots have been heavily farmed. Many age old upland pastures were managed as arable fields from the Bronze Age to medieval times and have only recently, perhaps over the last 200 years, reverted to grassland. Because of the Border Wars, when the hills were a buffer between hostile kingdoms, or a lawless wasteland picked over by reivers, the high hills were slow to change. Modern farming methods also failed to affect the area and the complex network of Bronze Age, Iron Age, Romano-British, Dark Age and medieval field systems and dwellings lie intact beneath a thin veneer of grass. Nowhere in Britain is there such an exciting historic landscape, largely unexplored and unexcavated; a demonstration of continuity in an age of change.

EACH WALK begins with an accurate assessment of its length in kilometres and miles, a brief description of the terrain and an estimate of the time it is likely to take to complete, assuming a few distractions along the way. All the walks are circular varying in length from 6.5km (4 miles) to 14.5km (9 miles). Families of moderate fitness should feel confident of attempting most routes with only a little preparation.

STARTING POINTS are from a suitable car parking space, either a formal parking area with a hard surface or a road verge wide enough to accommodate two or three cars at a time.

ALL ROUTES have been checked and signposts, stiles and waymarks provided where necessary. Occasionally a way-marking change in a section of the route may be met along the way. Unforseen but necessary alterations of this kind are carried out with as little inconvenience as possible to walkers.

THE ROUTE SYMBOLS on the maps are as follows: Right of Way ━━━━━

Permissive Path ▬ ▬ ▬ ▬ ▬

INTERPRETIVE NOTES are printed in the text in normal type, whilst route directions are given in bold type. GR refers to the Ordnance Survey grid reference system. Details on how to use this are printed on the 1:25,000 Pathfinder series of maps and on the 1:50,000 Landranger series. Sheets 74, 75, 80 and 81 (Landranger) cover all the walks in this publication. Please note that the map extracts used in this book are from the most recent series of OS Pathfinder which may not include some changes to fence-lines, plantations etc, although these features may be mentioned in the route descriptions.

COMFORT AND SAFETY are essential considerations when preparing for a walk.

Heavy boots and woollen socks used to be the recommended footwear, but these days there are better alternatives. Go for something that is lightweight and fully water-proof, supports the ankle and has a non-slip sole. Carry a rucksack and pack a sweater or fleece and waterproof jacket. The ruck-sack can be used for spare clothing, plasters, midge repellent and food. The sweater and waterproof are an acknowledgement that you are out on the hills; even in summer there can be a cold wind.

LOOK AFTER THE COUNTRYSIDE; it is in all our interests to do so. Walkers have a responsibility to leave the landscape as they find it and follow the Country Code. In particular, fasten all gates, keep to the recognised route and take any litter home. Most of the walks follow recognised foot-paths or bridleways but there are occasions when no rights of way exist and the path is by the permission of the landowner or farmer. Please be considerate when passing houses or crossing farmland, leave machinery and livestock alone, and if you wish to take a dog, keep it under control, preferably on a lead.

'A Hyeway For The Theefe'

Mounthooly – Red Cribs – The Schil – Fleehope Burn.
8.5km (5½ miles); ascent 400m (1312 feet); about 4 hours

This walk, which includes a section of the Pennine Way, is in the College Valley, one of the loveliest valleys in Northumberland and some say the most unspoilt. The first part along the valley floor is easy but thereafter the going is quite tough. The temptation to pause frequently and admire the view as you climb Red Cribs and The Schil will disguise any need to stop and draw breath. The two descents are steep and can be taxing on the knees but for all that it's a grand walk and an experience not to be missed – provided you are reasonably fit.

To reach the start at Mounthooly you need a permit to take the car beyond Hethpool. The College Valley is privately owned but about 12 cars a day are allowed up the valley except at lambing time, mid-April to the end of May. Permits are free and can be obtained from Sale and Partners, Estate Agents, 18-20 Glendale Road, Wooler NE71 6DN.

Leave the A697 at Akeld and follow the B6351 to Kirknewton (about 7km/4½ miles). Continue for another 1.5km to West Newton then turn left between the farm buildings onto a single track road signed Hethpool. Drive carefully up the valley to Hethpool. Keep on for another 6km (4 miles) past the farms of Whitehall and Fleehope until you reach the gate across the road 200m before Mounthooly. Park on the grass verge on the right (GR 882228).

Walk along the road, go through the gate, then bear right past the back of the shepherd's house and on along the track. Go through several gates to pass the conifer plantation and sheep pens.

In 1994 the College Valley Estates decided to fell the three large coniferous plantations near the head of the valley and replant the lower slopes with deciduous trees. The conifers were planted after the Second World War to provide shelter for stock. The accepted practice in those days was to create uniform blocks of fast-growing woodland without concern for either tree species or the landscape. Now in keeping with more enlightened forestry policies, some landowners are replanting exclusively with native broadleaved trees. Although it will be many years before they mature, these native trees are natural to the landscape and ultimately will provide a more varied wildlife habitat and a blaze of colour in the autumn.

Continue along the valley floor past a sheep stell next to the track.

To the left of the track the College Burn cuts its way down the valley, past steep-sided, scree-covered hills. In winter months rocky outcrops high on the hillsides are subject to the processes of freezing and thawing over many years. The surface breaks down and becomes unstable. The wintry weather continues to work on the scree making it constantly mobile and creating a slow downhill movement. Not many plants can gain a foothold among the rolling stones. Tracks across the valley sides are the result of generations of sheep using the same regular routes.

Carry on. In due course the burn and track run close together. Just before a sheep stell is reached turn right at the fork in the track. Head towards the red scar on the hillside in the distance.

The College Valley at Mounthooly

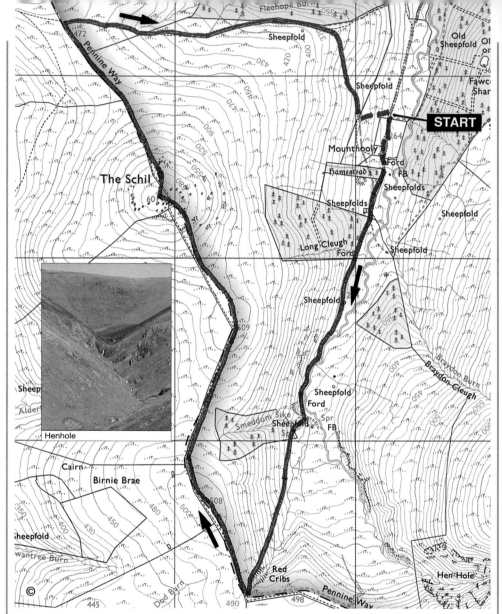

The map shows various features including:

START

Pennine Way, 472, Sheepfold, Flechope Burn, Old Sheepfold, Fawc... Shar..., Mounthooly, Ford, Homestead, FB, The Schil, Sheepfolds, Sheepfold, Long Cleugh, Ford, 509, Sheepfold, Braydon Burn, Braydon Cleugh, Sheep, Alder, Henhole, Cairn, Birnie Brae, 508, Sheepfold, Ford, Smeddum Sike, Spr, FB, 502, Sheepfold, wantree Burn, 445, Dod Burn, 490, 498, Red Cribs, Pennine Way, Hen Hole

The steep gully is Red Cribs; red, after the colour of the volcanic soil exposed by erosion, but the derivation of Cribs is anyone's guess. The gully was mentioned in Border papers dated 1597 as 'Gribbheade a passage and hyeway for the theefe'. Water forget-me-nots grow along the damp margins of the little burns that drain the rough pasture at the head of the valley. Forget-me-nots flower from June onwards, the flowers are blue sometimes fading to pink. The forget-me-not symbolizes constancy, true love and remembrance. There's a rather sad tale of how it got its name. A romantic young knight was attempting to pick these flowers which were growing on the edge of a fast-flowing river when he slipped and fell in. He managed to throw them to his ladylove standing on the bank and as he was swept to his death he called out 'Forget me not'.

Follow the path as it climbs steeply up the right side of Red Cribs.

The massive bulk of Cheviot at 815m (2674 feet) the highest hill in Northumberland, looms on the left. 'Out of the southest p'te of the said mountaine springeth and descendeth a lytle ryv'called Colledge'says Henry VIII's Border Survey, 1541. The 'lytle ryv' rises above Henhole, the gorge on Cheviot's flank and cascades down in a series of waterfalls. Henhole was formed thousands of years ago during a period of climatic regression known as the Little Ice Age, when small glaciers reappeared in the Cheviots. The distinctive circular hollow (corrie) above the gorge was gouged out by the ice and the gorge below by meltwater when the glaciers retreated as the climate warmed up.

Some slopes in Henhole face north and often a small patch of snow, a 'snow egg', will linger here into midsummer. Because it is so dark and deep, Henhole has entered local folklore as a place of magic and mystery. It is reputed to be inhabited by fairies and any human enticed into the gorge by their enchanting song may never get out again.

At the top of Red Cribs keep straight on to the fence marking the Border between England and Scotland. The path running alongside is the Pennine Way.

400m to the left is a refuge hut, providing shelter for walkers on one of the wildest and most remote stretches of the Pennine Way. The refuge, erected by National Park Voluntary Wardens in 1989, replaced an old railway carriage which had succumbed to the weather. The new shelter was prefabricated at the National Park Centre at Ingram in the Breamish Valley and was flown up by helicopter from RAF Boulmer together with all the timber cladding, roofing materials, concrete mixer and even water to mix the cement!

Turn right and follow the Pennine Way to the stile at the foot of The Schil.

From the Pennine Way there are extensive views down into the College Valley and across the Border into Scotland. It's a windswept area but one plant that grows quite happily in the peaty acidic conditions up here is harestail cottongrass. It has a single flower stem, with a pale yellow tufty head which appears in early spring. The seeds, like wisps of down, form a sea of white on the bleak moors and bogs in midsummer.

Cross the stile and climb to the rocky summit of The Schil 601m (1972 feet).

The stiff climb is worth all the effort for the view from the top. Across the head of the College

Hare Law from the ascent to The Schil

Border Ridge from The Schil

Valley is Cheviot summit with Henhole and Auchope Cairn on the extreme right. Left of Cheviot there are views into the Bellyside and Lambden Burns with the gable of Goldscleugh farmhouse standing out white in the landscape. Beyond Goldscleugh, in the far distance, are the hills and moorland around Eglingham and Chillingham. To the left of Goldscleugh, given a clear day, you should be able to see Bamburgh Castle and the Farne Islands on the horizon and in the middle distance Wester Tor on the right-hand side of the College Valley. Slightly left again you are looking across the rolling foothills of the Cheviots to the Milfield Plain. Moving round, the Tweed Basin lies due north while Scotland and the valley of the Bowmont Water are on the left, completing the circle.

There are several large areas of great woodrush growing on the summit and flanks of The Schil. Woodrush has long, glossy green leaves turning orange-brown in autumn. Like cottongrass, it is tolerant of acid soils but, as its name implies, it is commonly associated with woodland. Its presence on this exposed hillside suggests that at sometime in the valley's long history, scrub woodland may have existed at this altitude.

Leave the summit and keeping the fence on your left make your way downhill. Cross the stile in the fence and continue on until you reach a ladder stile and fingerpost by the wall. Take the route to the right signed Mounthooly 1½ miles. Walk on, gradually bearing right towards the fence about 180m

to the right. The path is indistinct but keep on over the source of the Fleehope Burn, until you come to the gate in the fence.

In late July the rank heather and bracken here is usually home to a family of whinchat. The parents' call is a weak 'chink' often followed by a buzzing note from the youngsters which is their contact call with the adults. By the second week in August the parents will have departed leaving the young to fend for themselves and find their own way to North Africa to overwinter.

Go through the gate and bear left on a narrow path across rough ground. Keep the conifer plantation on your left.

In summer you may notice globules of froth clinging to plant stems along the way. This is cuckoo-spit formed by the larvae of frog-hoppers, an aptly named bug which leaps like a frog and in some species vaguely resembles one too. Frog-hoppers are plant-suckers. The larvae suspend themselves on a plant, puncture it with piercing mouthparts then suck out the juices. To protect themselves from dehydration and from predators, air is forced into its own liquid waste creating a cocoon of bubbles, cuckoo-spit.

Just after passing a sheep stell on the hillside to the right, you reach a farm track. Follow the track as it bears right away from the plantation and winds steeply downhill towards Mounthooly. Go through the gate, turn left and continue down to the car park.

Kirknewton – Hethpool Bell – Torleehouse – Old Yeavering. 7km (4½ miles); ascent 150m (492 feet); about 3 hours

A pleasant meander along the picturesque banks of the College Burn, to the foot of Hethpool Bell. A gentle climb out of the valley, returning by farm tracks and a quiet country road. There's plenty of wildlife interest, including the possibility of seeing a herd of wild goats which live in the Cheviot Hills. For most of the route conditions underfoot are firm. Try to make time at the beginning or end of the walk to visit Kirknewton Church. It is one of the most important ecclesiastical buildings in Northumberland.

Park on the wide grass verge beside the B6351, near Kirknewton Church and the school playing field (GR 914303). Walk along the main road past the junction and the church on the left.

Kirknewton lies close to the confluence of the River Glen, the Bowmont Water and the College Burn. It's a tiny hamlet, dominated by the towering heights of the Cheviot Hills nearby.

St. Gregory's just across the road from where you parked is one of the most interesting churches in Northumberland. It is an unusual building. The exterior is 19th century, but there is more to this church than meets the eye. More impressive than the magnificent nave designed by the famous 19th century architect John Dobson, and the 12th century sculpture of the Adoration of the Magi, are the tunnel-vaulted chancel and south transept. Built in a more brutal period, their strength and solidity suggest that this church was a safe refuge for the local population in times of great danger.

The graveyard has several interesting headstones. Among them is that of Josephine Butler a great social reformer. She worked tirelessly throughout the late 19th century to rehabilitate young girls who for one reason or another had been forced into prostitution. She also campaigned for women to have the vote.

Continue on until you reach some imposing red sandstone walls and buildings on the right.

This was Kirknewton Station, built when the London North Eastern Railway Company (L.N.E.R.) opened a branch line from Alnwick to Coldstream in 1887.

You can still see the track bed of the old railway to the right where for a short distance it runs close to the road.

Most of the line's income came from carrying agricultural goods – livestock, potatoes and grain. There were no large communities along the route to provide enough passengers to make the railway profitable. It was competition from the motor-bus, which was able to go into all the villages and hamlets by-passed by the railways, that forced the company to withdraw passenger services in 1930. The Wooler to Coldstream section of the line continued to carry goods until it was axed in 1965. With the closure of the line to passengers however, the well-designed stone-built stations were sold off and converted into attractive country homes.

Walk on to the far side of the bridge over the College Burn. Go over the stone step stile on your left by the fingerpost signed Hethpool and follow the path through the tall vegetation.

Special branch-line train headed by loco. No. 46474 entering Kirknewton station on service from Tweedmouth to Wooler (date unknown)

The Cheviot burns respond rapidly to heavy rainfall and winter thaws; the level rises and falls very quickly as the surface water drains away. Turbulent floods churn up stones in the burns, producing the rounded boulders and gravel beds typical of these water courses.

Here, the gravel beds have been colonised by broom and gorse whose root systems have helped stabilise the loose stones. This in turn has provided suitable conditions for other plants to move in, among them mullein and St. John's wort. St. John's wort is dedicated to St. John the Baptist whose feast day is June 24th. It was said that if it was gathered that morning while still covered in dew, it would ward off the Evil Eye, ghosts, goblins, fire and thunderbolts!

Mullein with its tall spike of yellow flowers and soft, grey-green leaves, is less common along this stretch than it used to be, because it is being shaded out by the taller and denser shrubs.

Cross the step stile and carry on along the bankside. After about 350m the path leaves the burnside and goes uphill. Climb the stile over the fence and, keeping the fence on your left go on to the ladder stile. Cross back over the fence here and bear right, gradually making your way downhill to the haughland.

This land is part of West Kirknewton Farm. It's a small hill farm by Cheviot standards, 583 hectares (1439 acres) raising sheep and cattle. For most of the year the cattle graze the hillslopes but in winter they are brought down to the haugh to be fed. The fact that the ground is well-drained is an advantage because it is less likely to be turned into a quagmire by trampling hooves.

Keeping the burn on your left, continue over the haughland for 500m through a gate on the valley floor then follow the track uphill. Walk through the gate at the top of the bank and on to a ladder stile in the wall. Go over the stile and follow the path as it contours around the hill just above the trees.

In co-operation with the landowner, the semi-natural oak woodland on the left has been fenced off by the National Park to allow young trees and woodland plants to become re-established. The old trees are particularly attractive to green and great spotted

Towards Westnewton from near Hethpool Linn

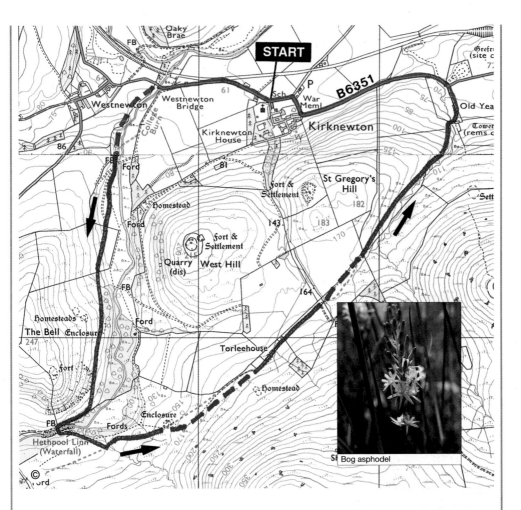

Bog asphodel

woodpeckers; holes excavated by them in the decaying trunks make excellent nesting sites. 280 different kinds of insects are reputed to live on the oak tree, so woodpeckers and tree creepers have an abundant supply of food right on their doorstep!

The oak woodland is also the site of a large rookery. In early spring the rooks begin to nest-build, carrying twigs, calling and displaying. By April – May there's a lot more activity with adults carrying food to their young. If there is a dry spring, the rooks will have problems because the ground will be hard and dry and the usual food for their nestlings, earthworms and leather jackets, will be well down out of reach. If that happens, the youngsters may suffer a higher death rate.

Carry on alongside the woodland fence to the stile in the fence on the left.

A lot of the humps and bumps on this dry, sandy slope are anthills. You may notice that some have been excavated; this is either badger or green woodpecker digging into the anthill in search of ant grubs or pupae.

In amongst the anthills are numerous small self-set hawthorns, varying in size from about 1 to 2 metres high. A glance at these hawthorns will show a clear browse line. This is caused by sheep nibbling at the young twigs and leaves. Once the tree gets above sheep height it is able to bush out. It is interesting to compare the level of the browse line on this side of the valley with that on the opposite side where the grazing habits of the wild goats have raised it.

Cross the stile and continue on keeping the fence on your right.

You are now in the fenced-off woodland enclosure which has been restocked mainly with oak saplings to help recolonise what was a large clearing.

At the corner of the fence go straight on downhill to meet a fence. Turn right and continue on keeping the fence on your left to reach a stile. Cross the stile and with the fence now on your right carry on going slightly uphill to cross another stile.

The hill on the right is Hethpool Bell. The trees growing round the top are the Collingwood oaks. Admiral Collingwood fought with Nelson at the Battle of Trafalgar in 1805 and although the Hethpool estate was not his main home, he planted the oaks in the hope that they would produce fine timber for the country's ships. Lacking a rich, deep soil and blasted by winds the trees have become stunted and deformed.

Straight ahead is Hethpool House built in 1919. Lying at the bottom of the garden and smothered in ivy, are the ruins of a much earlier building. A stronghold was recorded here in 1415. It was certainly needed because Hethpool suffered frequent raids by Scottish reivers. In one instance in 1596 a reiving band of Kerrs, Youngs and Burns attacked the hamlet, killed one of the tenants and made off with 40 cows and oxen.

Walk on for a few metres and turn left to the footbridge over the College Burn.

The burn flows through a steep-sided gorge with a number of waterfalls. Deciduous trees cling to the banks and ferns retain a hold in the cooler, shaded crevices in the rocks.

Throughout the year brown trout lie up in the deep, peaty pools. They seem to suspend themselves in the water, gently moving with the pace of the current ready to rise to the surface to catch any insects that have fallen into the burn higher up.

Brown trout

Sneezewort

At the far side of the bridge turn left. Follow the path between the trees and cross the step stile over the fence. Turn right and make your way uphill to where the ground levels out by the wooded banks of a little burn to the left.

A wet area near the path contains a luxuriant growth of damp-loving plants, marsh thistle, bog asphodel, heath-spotted orchid, greater birdsfoot trefoil and sneezewort which was used in the past to make snuff – hence its name!

The hillsides ahead were covered in bracken. Before the bracken was sprayed it presented a serious problem for the shepherd who had difficulty in finding his sheep when it was at its height in summer. Spraying controls the bracken and has positive benefits for wildlife habitats such as heather moorland and flower-rich banksides, which would otherwise be under threat from this rapidly spreading fern.

Carry on to just before the gate.

From here, stand and scan the steep slopes; you may be lucky enough to spot the wild goats. Goats have been roaming these hills since pre-medieval times. The name of the nearby hill Yeavering Bell is derived from the Anglo-Saxon Gefrin meaning 'hill of the goats'. Individuals are difficult to pick out against the rocky hillside because their colour, mainly grey and dark brown, provides excellent camouflage. The billys have a thick neck, a long 'goatee' beard and an impressive set of horns, scimitar-shaped and curving outwards at the end. The nannys give birth by mid-March, usually a single kid, but there's often a high mortality rate among the young as wintry weather can last well into spring in these hills. As a result, numbers remain stable at around 20 to 25.

Turn left. Walk downhill, cross the burn, go up the other side and bear right to the step stile over the electric fence. Cross the stile and continue uphill through the field making for the square stone stell about 300m ahead.

The stell stands next to the remains of an ancient farming settlement. The people who lived here 2000 years ago shepherded the hills much as their descendants do today.

They built round houses from boulders picked up from the hillsides and surrounded them with a stock-proof bank of earth and stone. Have a look at the site and try to visualise what life was like for the people who once lived there.

Join the farm track nearby and follow it uphill. Go through the gate into the conifer plantation and leave by the gate at the far side. Carry on along the track. Pass Torleehouse (renamed Kirknewton Tors) and, keeping straight on through several gates begin the long, gradual descent.

The hill to the right is Yeavering Bell. On the top is the largest prehistoric hillfort in Northumberland, over 5 hectares (12 acres). Within the stone wall which runs right round the summit are the hollows and level areas for 130 circular wooden houses.

Go through the gate just before the old farm building at the bottom of the track.

This was probably a 16th century bastle. Only the ground floor survives but the thick walls are typical bastle construction. The building was marked on old maps as King Edwin's palace of Ad Gefrin (Old Yeavering). Edwin who lived in the 7th century was the first Christian King of Northumbria. Excavation has shown that the actual site of his palace is half a mile east of where this track joins the tarmac road. A stone monument marking the site has been erected by the roadside.

Continue on through another gate and past the cottages.

The cottages are called Old Yeavering, probably because of their proximity to the remains of an earlier deserted village. William Hutchinson, historian and traveller who passed this way in 1776 to visit Yeavering Bell, described Yeavering as "a mean village, and little regarded by travellers, though once a place of royal residence." In summer meadow cranesbill grows in great profusion on the trackside verges. The density of the plants with their various shades of blue make a delightful end to the walk.

Continue to the main road. Turn left, and facing the oncoming traffic, return to Kirknewton.

On the track to Torleehouse >

Ponds, Plantations and an Old Lonnen

3

Humbleton – Gleadscleugh – Black Law – Gains Law.
10km (6½ miles); ascent 200m (656 feet); about 4½ hours

In spite of easy going underfoot for most of the way this is quite a strenuous walk. It includes one steep climb up the lower slopes of Harehope Hill, a long, gradual ascent from the bridge over the Akeld Burn and a section over rough ground. Nevertheless the views are magnificent; added interest is in the variety of scenery, wildlife and historic landscapes to appreciate en route.

The walk begins about 1.5km (1 mile) west of Wooler. To reach the start, leave the A697 at the junction signed Low Humbleton. Follow the narrow single-track road uphill for about 1km. Bear right at the next junction on the left and continue on to the end of the tarmac. Park on the grass verge on the right (GR 974283).

This is known locally as High Humbleton. Apart from the modernised cottages nearby, humps and bumps in the fields round about are the only indications that once there was a village here. In medieval days High Humbleton was large enough to have a church, a mill and a village green but times change; by the 19th century wealthy landowners were buying out smaller freeholders and when they and their families began to move away, High Humbleton gradually declined. Women from the surrounding area came into the village and broke up the headstones in the churchyard because the sandstone made excellent scouring blocks for cleaning hearths, floors and doorsteps.

Go through the field gate on the right next to the ruined cottage. Continue to the next gate and keep straight on.

Below, to the right of the track are the old mill ponds. The lower pond is partly drained and largely overgrown but it is still a wetland habitat

Yellow Iris

for water-loving plants such as marsh speedwell and various species of rushes and sedges. The upper pond is standing water, a good breeding place for frogs and damsel flies. During the summer months flowering yellow iris add a splash of colour to the fringes of the pond. In late autumn, the flowers are replaced by plump green pods like small cucumbers, bursting with bright orange seeds.

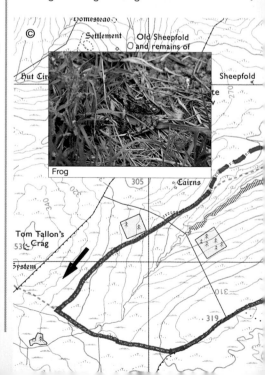
Frog

Pass the scree-covered slopes of Humbleton Hill on the left and at the fork in the track bear right. Continue on a short distance, then leave the track where it bends left and turn right down the slope to the large tree by the wall. Turn left and, keeping the wall on your right, continue on.

The small plantation and wetland area on the far side of the wall is a National Park conservation project carried out by field staff and Voluntary Wardens after a grant-aided agreement was negotiated with the landowner. Willow and alder have been planted in the damper areas and ash, oak and Scots pine on the drier ground. The old mill race running through the plantation has been dammed to create a wetland habitat for marsh plants, invertebrates and birds.

The fenced-off area excludes sheep which would otherwise damage the young trees; as a result the grass grows tall and rank. This in turn offers a home for field voles, the prey of short-eared owls which fly during the day and for kestrels that often hover over the plantation in search of food.

At the end of the wall go past the field gate then through the wicket gate where the fence and the wall meet. Bear half left and head towards two large boulders.

The bank and ditch to the right of the path are part of the former mill race which ran along the lower slopes of Monday Cleugh and Humbleton Hill to the mill ponds at High Humbleton. From the early 17th to the early 19th centuries a large number of water-powered corn mills operated in the uplands. They produced flour and meal from barley and oats, the only cereals which would grow successfully at reasonably high altitudes. The head race, usually man-made, and fed by small burns, sikes and run-off from the hills, had to be of considerable length to supply the force required to turn the wheel. Sluice gates were sometimes provided to regulate the flow and feeder ponds to supplement the water supply.

Where the mill race bends round to the left, walk straight along to the gate in the wall ahead. Cross the stile beside the gate and continue uphill. Pause for breath at the corner of the wall on the right.

To the right, over the red roofs of Bendor, stretches the Milfield Plain and the fertile valley of the River Till. It's a peaceful scene now but about 600 years ago, on September 13th 1402, opposing English and Scottish armies fought a bitter and bloody battle in the fields around Bendor. The Scots under Archibald, Earl of Douglas had taken up a strong position

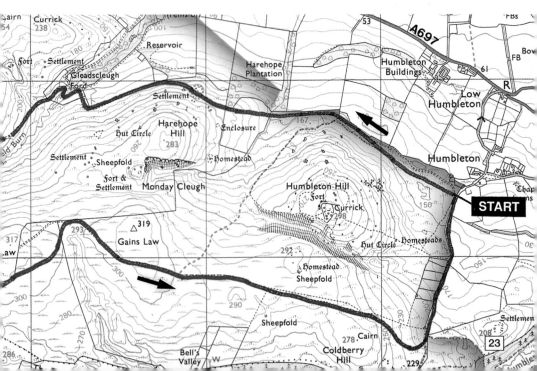

on the slopes of Humbleton Hill but they were no match for the English archers who shot uphill with deadly effect. The battle ended in victory for the English and their leader, Harry (Hotspur) Percy gained revenge for his humiliating defeat by the Scots at the Battle of Otterburn in 1388. The site of the Battle of Homildon (Humbleton) Hill is marked by a large boulder, probably a prehistoric standing stone, two fields to the right of Bendor and a short distance from the A697. You may see the stone from the viewpoint provided the field is not under a standing crop.

Continue on and cross the stile next to the wicket gate. Follow the path as it contours around the slopes of Harehope Hill.

Down to the right, on the bend of the A697, is Akeld. Like High Humbleton it was once a fair-sized village then, after land changes in the 19th century, it became a large farm with labourers' cottages. Today all the farm build-ings have been converted into luxury holiday accommodation, an indication of how modern farming is thriving on diversity.

Carry on as the path gradually begins to descend the hill to run alongside the wall on the right.

The three parallel strands of wire on top of the wall are 'jump wires.' In most sheep flocks certain individuals have the dexterity to jump any height of wall. For these ewes and their offspring who are quick to learn, the grass is always greener on the other side of the fence. Hay and silage crops in inbye fields and young plantations have to be protected. The wire strands heighten the barrier and provide an additional deterrent to these would-be climbers.

Go through the gate and follow the wall as it turns sharp right downhill.

The solitary house in the valley bottom is Gleadscleugh. It used to be a pair of cottages for shepherds who worked in the hills around here. The tradition of shepherding sheep and herding cattle in these parts goes back more than 2,000 years but in those days people lived on higher, drier ground with a good view. Ahead, on the opposite side of the valley is a narrow promontory protected on the right by a steep-sided valley, Glead's Cleugh. This is the site of a prehistoric settlement with several house platforms and space to corral animals safely at night.

Cross the stile by the gate. Bear left and continue downhill to meet a track. Turn left

and follow the track round to cross the Akeld burn by the bridge.

There used to be extensive bracken beds on Harehope Hill and up the Akeld Burn. These grew quite tall in summer; they reduced grazing areas and were a hindrance to the shepherd when looking for his sheep. Spraying has helped to reduce the spread of bracken and where it has died back, a number of plants have re-colonised the area, notably foxgloves.

Foxgloves

In summer the flowers grow from a central spike in the middle of a large, green, rather wrinkled rosette of leaves. The lower lip of each flower is covered in coarse white hairs which prevent small insects climbing in and stealing nectar without working for the plant in return by pollinating the flowers. The reproductive organs are on the upper part of the tubular flower, so pollination requires a large insect like a bumble bee gaining entry, getting its back 'scrubbed' and carrying the pollen away to another flower.

Continue up the slope until you meet another track. Turn left, go through the gate and begin the long walk uphill. At the top of the hill the track forks. Take the left fork, continue on through another gate across the track and past a small conifer plantation on the right.

Keep to the track which becomes grassy and wet in places. Go through the next gate at the corner of the conifer wood on the left. Turn left and follow the track through the gate and around to where it goes over a small burn. Cross the burn and turn left to leave the track. Head off on the clear path across rough ground to the gateway in the wall on the skyline. At the gateway stop and look back at the view.

To the right, the broad conical hill is Yeavering Bell. The summit is ringed by the remains of a stone wall enclosing the largest Iron Age hillfort in Northumberland. Within the wall are over 130 platforms for timber houses. To the left of Yeavering is Tom Tallon's Crag; who Tom Tallon was, no one knows. Ahead, the flat-topped hill over the ridge is Easter Tor and the long hill with the rock-like point at one end is Wester Tor.

Do not go through the gateway but turn left and carry on keeping the wall immediately on your right. Go through the gate where the wall and the fence meet, continue on and go through the next gate. The wall is now on your left.

View towards Bendor and Fenton

Red grouse

This area of heather land is a grouse moor. As you are walking you may hear the characteristic call of the red grouse which sounds like 'go back, go back'. If frightened it will rise suddenly, skimming away with intermittent glides in low level flight across the heather.

You may also come across occasional stones or upturned sods of peat sprinkled with what appears to be whitish gravel. This is quartz grit, put out by gamekeepers in areas of

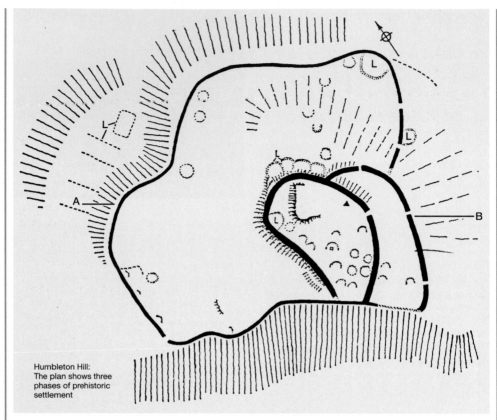

Humbleton Hill:
The plan shows three
phases of prehistoric
settlement

peaty ground where there is insufficient natural grit. The red grouse stores the grit in its gizzard where it is used to break up heather shoots before the food can be digested.

At the corner of the wall, the path forks. Take the less obvious path straight on through the heather to a stile in the post and wire fence. Cross the stile and walk on to the ruined wall. Turn right. Continue on the broad track as it bears right around Gains Law. As the track levels out pause and look over to Humbleton Hill on the left.

Other than having the advantage of a tremendous view, no one today would consider living on Humbleton Hill. Yet all the evidence shows that in prehistoric times it was a favoured place for permanent habitation. The original settlement had at least eleven round timber houses sheltered by an enclosure wall 4 metres thick. Two extensions, terracing for crops and burial cairns point to continuous occupation over a long period. 'The Celtic population of these hills seems to have been

very large' wrote W. W. Tomlinson in his Comprehensive Guide to Northumberland, 1888. Perhaps it was climatic change to cooler, wetter conditions that finally drove people down from the hills to the valley floor.

Go through the field gate across the green track, on along the ridge and then downhill. Follow the track as it turns left at the bottom of the hill, through the field gate ahead and continue down to your car.

The last part of the walk is down an old lonnen. These leafy lanes were well-used tracks linking farms, hamlets and villages in times past. Many have disappeared from the landscape in the past 100 years. The National Park has grant-aided a tree planting scheme to ensure that this lonnen will survive. Ash, beech and cherry have been planted to fill existing gaps and to replace dying trees. As they mature they will add variety to the landscape, provide a more diverse habitat for wildlife and make a very pleasant end to this route for the next generation of hill walkers.

Wooler Common Picnic Site – Hellpath – Common Burn.

11.5 km (7½ miles); ascent 250m (820 feet); about 4½ hours

One of the loveliest walks in the whole of the National Park at any time of year, but particularly in late July – early August when the heather moors are at their best. The outward route is on well-defined grassy tracks and paths; the return is on a metalled bridleway. There are no steep climbs, conditions under-foot are good and the scenery is superb.

The starting place is about 1.5km (1 mile) south west of Wooler. To get there, leave the market place by Ramsey's Lane and keep straight on along the Common Road until you reach the far end of the picnic site. Park on the grass just before the bridge (GR 977272).

The Humbleton Burn Valley has always been a popular place for walks and picnics. This picnic site was laid out by the Forestry Commission in 1980. It is one of an increasing number of recreational facilities for the general public on Forestry land. Since one fifth of the National Park is owned by Forest Enterprise (part of the Forestry Commission), these facilities are welcomed by the Park Authority.

Keeping the burn on your right, take the bridleway signed Wooler Common.

The area near the burn is a valuable wetland habitat. Heron, moorhen and grey wagtail are regularly seen feeding here. In summer the water's edge is ablaze with the bright yellow flowers of mimulus, commonly known as monkey flower because its intricately folded petals resemble the face of a monkey. Mimulus was introduced into this country from Alaska in the early 19th century. It escaped from gardens and is now so widespread along the burns in the Cheviot valleys that it is regarded as a wild flower.

Cross the stile and follow the track as it

winds uphill. Near the top of the hill bear half-right at the fingerpost signed Wooler Common. Walk towards the cottage seen ahead. Go past the cottage and cross the stile in the fence by the fingerpost signed Broadstruther. After 20m cross another stile and turn right. Keeping the fence on your right walk downhill to cross the stile by the gate. With the derelict wall on your right continue on towards the plantation.

The fields around Wooler Common Farm are all down to permanent pasture and several are infested with thistles. To most people, a thistle is a thistle but as with many other plants, there are different species. In these fields, there is spear thistle, a tall spiny plant with large, reddish-purple flowerheads, creeping thistle with fragrant, pale-lilac flowers and meadow thistle – the least prickly – with single flower-heads. When the flowers have been pollinated flocks of brightly-coloured goldfinch descend on the seed heads. Gentle breezy days in August produce clouds of thistle-down, which is bad news for farmers because the thistles spread further afield.

At the corner of the plantation, stop and look back.

Half-left, beyond the gap in the hills lies the Milfield Plain, an extensive tract of low-lying land of great geological and economic importance. After the last Ice Age the plain was covered by a huge lake. When it drained away, vast areas of silt, sand and gravel deposited over a long period of time were left exposed. The sand and gravel have been excavated by quarry companies while the fertile silt still yields heavy crops of grain.

Follow the track along the edge of the plantation and continue on in the same direction across the open moorland.

Mimulus

4

View towards Wooler Common

The stones and boulders to the right have, over the years, rolled down from the scree slopes above; many are covered in a range of different lichens. The most common is the map lichen (rhizocapon geographicum), so called because of the tracery of black lines and dots across its yellow-green surface.

Go through the wicket gate and turn right along the Carey Burn to its confluence with the Broadstruthers Burn on the left.

This is where the Broadstruthers Burn joins the Common Burn. Together they flow on as the Carey Burn. The woodland on the banks of the Broadstruthers Burn is Luckenarks Wood, one of the few remaining semi-natural woods in the National Park. Centuries of grazing have prevented natural regeneration of these old woodlands and now they cover a mere one percent of the land in the National Park. Luckenarks Wood includes alder, birch, hazel, rowan and willow. The area has been fenced off from sheep to allow the woodland to regenerate.

Carry on to the bridge. Cross over and take the path up the slope on the right. Continue on, keeping the fence on your right and the valley of the Broadstruthers Burn on your left. Follow the path along the hillside, go through two wicket gates and after about 20m, turn right onto the path and go uphill. Towards the top, turn and look back at the view.

This is the heart of Cheviot country, wild and empty. Left of The Cheviot is Broadhope Hill and below that, the cluster of deciduous trees hides the ruins of Broadstruther Farm. Continuing further along, the low summit under Hedgehope Hill is Blackseat Hill, then well to the left again is Cold Law.

Keep straight on, climb two stiles and into a small plantation. Follow the path through the trees to the end of the plantation. Cross two stiles near one another and continue on a narrow path towards Commonburn House.

Much of this area is now managed as a grouse moor. There are fewer sheep and the heather cover, damaged by over-grazing is recovering. As a result the moorland has greater conservation value for ground-nesting birds such as grouse, curlew and golden plover.

In summer the flowering heather feeds numerous insects – bees, wasps, flies and moths. The spectacular caterpillars of northern eggar and emperor moths are surprisingly

Beyond the plantation, the hill to the left is Hart Heugh, ahead and to the right is the rugged face of Watch Hill, and right of that are the wooded slopes of Fredden Hill. The area may look inhospitable now but 3000 years ago Bronze Age farming communities worked this land. The remains of their field systems and their burial cairns can still be seen on the moor.

Go through the wicket gate into the plantation and on down Hellpath.

Hellpath is an evocative name especially as the way is downhill but not to Hell, only to the valley bottom. In fact Hellpath is probably a corruption of hill path. To the left there are tremendous views down the steep-sided valley of the Carey Burn and ahead, at the top of the Broadstruthers Burn, is The Cheviot with Preston Hill and Great Moor in the foreground.

The hillslopes on both sides of the path are very dry; in many places the soil itself is exposed. A number of insects prefer dry habitats. If you come this way in summer and sit on the bankside for a while, you should see ants scurrying over the ground and perhaps grasshoppers laying their eggs in the sandy soil.

Some plants thrive in conditions like this, particularly bell heather, bilberry, woodsage and tormentil. The exposed edge has also allowed broom to come in. It is a pioneering species. Much of it is reaching maturity but there are new plants springing up. Broom is a member of the pea family and by August the flowers have been replaced by black pods. When a pod dries, it splits and twists with an explosive 'crack', flinging out the seeds which germinate on new ground away from the parent plant. In this way broom is able to spread over a wide area.

Pause at the bottom of Hellpath.

The Carey Burn from Hellpath

difficult to see, despite being more than 7cm long. The black and ginger northern eggar caterpillar is covered in short, spikey hairs (which can cause a rash if touched), whilst the emperor is camouflaged in green with black stripes and pink warts. On sunny afternoons these caterpillars are much easier to see because they like to climb to the top of the heather and bilberry bushes or sunbathe alongside the path.

Cross the Common Burn. If in spate, use the footbridge to the right.

The Common Burn rises on the saddle between Hare Law and Coldburn Hill. Upland burns complete the beautiful and varied scenery of the Cheviots. The clear, fast-flowing waters provide a habitat for the aquatic larvae or nymphs of mayfly, stonefly and caddisfly. They feed on whatever is washed down in the current, but to avoid being dislodged they need to be able to anchor themselves to boulders or stones. Mayfly and stonefly nymphs have flattened bodies, they scuttle around on the sheltered sides of the boulders and the current flows over them. Caddisfly larvae spin

Golden plover nest

webs of silk for protection and anchorage and to catch passing specks of food. In quieter backwaters, another kind of caddisfly larva makes a home out of sand grains, cementing them together into a tube to keep its soft body out of the way of frogs or fish.

Go through the gate in the wall. Bear left uphill towards the house. Go through the next gate, across the pasture to another gate between the cottage and the farm-house. Please walk quietly and keep dogs on a lead. Turn right onto the metalled bridleway and begin the long walk back to the picnic site. The route goes across moorland then through a conifer plantation.

The view to the left opens out across heather moorland. If a moor is to have any feeding value for sheep and grouse, it has to be properly managed. The most effective way of encouraging fresh growth is by burning.

"Muir burning" usually takes place in October when the fells are dry after the long summer or in March before ground-nesting birds lay their eggs. Small areas of moor are burnt over a 15 year cycle so that there is always a succession of nutritious young shoots for beast and bird alike. Scattered over the

"Muir burning"

moor are oval-shaped cairns built by earlier people who lived in these high hills. The cairns may be graves or simply heaps of stone piled up when the ground was cleared for cultivation. Beyond the moor, the far hillside is gouged by a number of deep, steep-sided dry valleys known as The Trows. They are glacial meltwater channels carved out by water flowing beneath a blanket of ice some 10,000 years ago.

After passing through a gate the track skirts another plantation to reach a cattle grid. Cross the grid. The route now continues as a fenced public road for about 2.5 km. Go past the cottages of Brown's Law, then Peter's Field to return to the parking area.

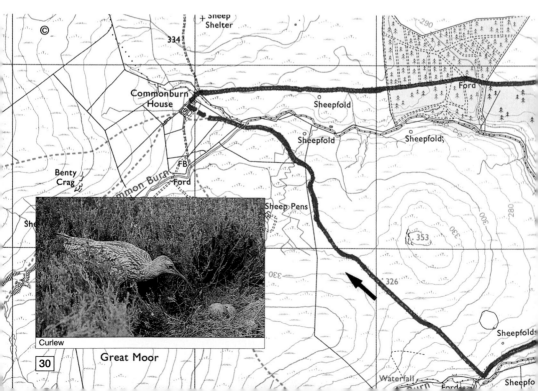

Curlew

30

Great Moor

Head of Trows Burn

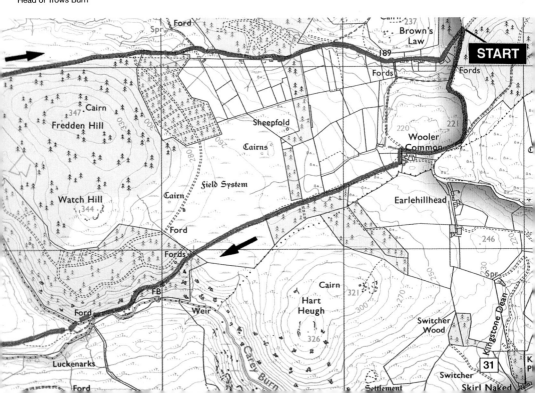

START

Ford
Spr
Cairn 237
Brown's
Law
189
Fords
Fords
Cairn 347
Fredden Hill
Sheepfold
220
221
Cairns
Wooler
Common
Watch Hill
344
Field System
Earlehillhead
Cairn
Ford
246
Fords
Cairn 321
FB
Cairn
Hart
Heugh
Ford
Weir
326
Switcher
Wood
Luckenarks
Carey Burn
Switcher
Ford
31
Settlement
Skirl Naked

Meet Four Burns

5

Carey Burn Bridge – Hawsen Burn – Broadstruther.
10.5km (7 miles); ascent 190m (623 feet); about 4-4½ hours

An outstanding walk, full of interest with an easy start along the valley floor. There's only one uphill section which isn't very strenuous, thereafter it's an airy walk over wild upland with a superlative view to finish. There is some wet ground to cross in the middle section otherwise the going is firm.

The starting place is about 4km (2½ miles) south west of Wooler. To get there, leave Wooler by Cheviot Street. Follow the signs to Earle and Middleton Hall then turn right for Langleeford. Park on the wide grass verge on the right just before Carey Burn Bridge, the first bridge in the valley (GR 976250). Cross the bridge and walk up the road.

The large agricultural building on the right, put up in the early 1980s, reflects the changes that have taken place in the management of stock. Cattle can be overwintered inside instead of being left on the hill. The slatted external wall ensures plenty of air circulates round the building to prevent pneumonia. For all their great size, continental breeds are more delicate than the hardier British breeds they are gradually replacing. This type of management makes life easier for the farmer. Cattle are taken off the soft land where their hooves destroy the grass, they are under cover and because they are confined can be fed more conveniently. The disadvantage is that the farmer needs to use heavy farm machinery to bring fodder and straw bedding to the stock and there's the additional problem of getting rid of accumulated slurry waste.

You may walk up the valley either on the road or on the pasture by the waterside. After passing Coronation Wood, the conifer plantation on the right, continue for about 1km to the cattle grid.

The hillside on the right is covered in scattered hawthorns one of the few trees to have

survived after the natural woodland has gone. Hawthorn is more resistant to sheep nibbling and can find enough nourishment in poor soils on stony ground to maintain a hold.

Three or four pairs of common sandpiper usually nest in the Harthope Valley. They arrive from North Africa in spring and establish their territory and nesting sites on broken ground by the water's edge where there's good visibility. The male attracts the female by lifting his wings to show the white underwing feathers. This is followed by a display with both birds flicking their wings and chasing each other over the water with a high-pitched, rolling trill.

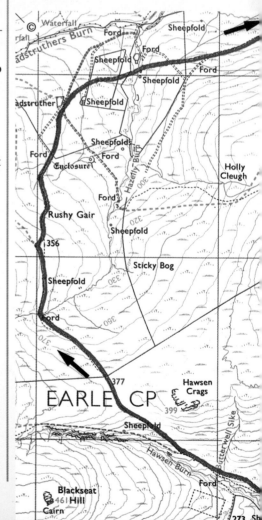

Cross the cattle grid and after a few metres stop near the noticeboard where the Backwood Burn comes in from the right.

The alder trees beside the burn have several holes in their trunks. It is easy to see which are the most recent – the ones where the bark has been stripped off round the edges leaving them clean. The holes have been made by a great spotted woodpecker. Its usual habit is to hack into the tree near a dead branch so there's only about an inch of good wood to go through before it is into soft rotting timber where it makes its flask-shaped nest cavity.

Keep on up the valley past the former shepherd's cottage at Langlee on the left.

The bracken beds in the Harthope Valley are a perfect habitat for whinchats. They too are summer visitors. Whinchats are sometimes confused with wheatears but they can often be distinguished by the way in which they perch on the bracken instead of on stones or walls and by their size and plumage. The whinchat is a smaller bird with a brown, streaked back and a dark eye stripe with a black line above. The male has a white v-shaped mark on its back and an orangy-pink upper breast.

There's also a reasonable chance of seeing a weasel darting about among the boulders in search of mice or young rabbits. Weasels look like slender cigars, are smaller than stoats and their short tail does not have a black tip.

Continue past a fingerpost by the road signed Cold Law. At the next fingerpost, signed Broadstruther and Goldscleugh,

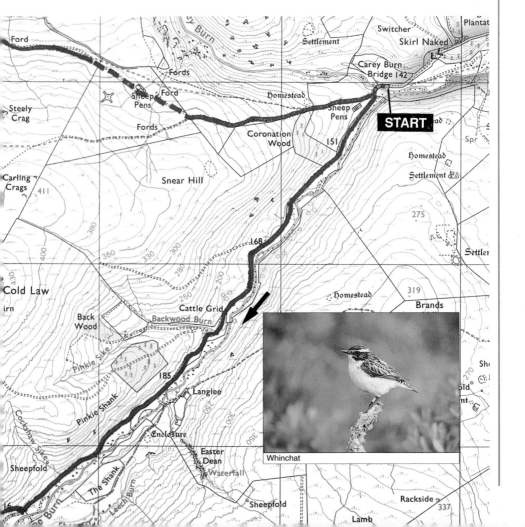

Whinchat

leave the tarmac road and go right uphill on the green track. Follow the track along the hillslope and just before it begins to descend towards a sheep stell, stop and turn right onto a narrow path up the side of the Hawsen Burn.

On the opposite side of the Harthope Valley on the skyline is a series of tors or rock pinnacles. The one with the double pinnacle is Langlee Crags; to the right, the next is Housey Crags, so called because from another angle it resembles a house with a sloping roof. The tors are formed of baked andesite, a rock that weathers at a slower rate than the granite core of the surrounding andesite and as a result, they have been left standing as craggy outcrops.

Ahead, the white painted house on the valley floor is Langleeford, to its left is Hedgehope Hill and to its right The Cheviot.

Follow the path above the burn to reach a junction of paths in just under 1km.

The isolated trees on the left bank of the Hawsen Burn are rowans, sometimes known as mountain ash. Rowan comes from the Scandinavian word 'raun' meaning a charm. For hundreds of years people have believed in the tree's power to protect them and their animals from witchcraft and evil spirits. Rowan planted near a house, or its wood used as a door lintel or roof rafters kept the occupants safe. Cows were protected by tethering pegs made of rowan, or by bunches of rowan hung over their stalls. Today, some folk believe the luckiest charm is a branch from a 'flying rowan' – one growing out of a cleft in another rowan tree.

Rowan is a characteristic tree of the uplands and is found throughout the National Park. With its creamy-white blossom in spring, brilliant red berries in late summer and colourful

Rowan

leaves in autumn it is a popular choice for tree-planting schemes for wildlife and its landscape value.

Bear right, away from the burn. Hawsen Crag is up on the right.

The Hawsen Burn is one of the few places in the Cheviots where in early spring you could see a bird resembling a blackbird but with a distinctive white crescent round its breast. This is a ring ouzel. Like the common sandpiper they also winter in North Africa and Southern Spain. The cock birds arrive in this country around March – April before the rowans are in leaf. They perch on the bare branches and sing loudly to proclaim their territory and to attract a mate.

The path eventually levels out and crosses poorly drained ground to reach a stile by the gate in the fence ahead.

The fence is the march (boundary) fence between two farms. The large stone by the fence just to the left is probably one of a series marking the boundary. During the late 18th – early 19th century period of agricultural improvement many landowners delineated their estate boundaries with stones inscribed with their initials. The letter S on one side of this stone probably refers to George Selby of Twisell, whose property in 1673 included 'Langleyford and Bradstrother'.

Go over the stile and follow the narrow path through the heather. After crossing a small burn bear right up to a corrugated iron hut. Pass to the left of the hut. The path becomes faint but continues in the direction of the crag on the skyline until the trees around the ruins of Broadstruther come into view.

This area is Rushy Gair and is aptly named. Gair means a strip of better quality grass but in this instance the rushes bear witness to the wet state of the ground.

Ring ouzel

Keep to the path as it descends through the heather and over the fell towards Broadstruther. Cross a deep drain and make for the gate in the fence ahead. Go through this gate and the next to reach the ruined house.

'Broadstroir' within the great 'forest of Chyvyot' is first mentioned in documents dated 1254. The derelict farmhouse, another former shepherd's dwelling, is of more recent date. Without the advantages of a tarmac road, four-wheel-drive vehicles, electricity and a telephone, life must have been extremely hard for the people who had to live here as recently as the 1950s.

Passing to the right of the house leave the track, bear right downhill on an ill-defined path and through the gateway in the wall ahead. Follow the path across rough pasture. Go through the gap in the next derelict wall and on to a gate in the fence overlooking the Hazelly Burn.

The Carey Burn

Go through the gate, follow the track downhill and cross the bridge. Turn right. After 20m turn left and head uphill around the quarry. Walk on for about 90m. Cross the farm track, go straight on and over the stile in the fenceline ahead. Continue onto the clear track and follow this to a gate. Go through the gate and on to another gate. Turn left through this gate.

The view from here is breathtaking. You are looking down the wooded slopes of Happy Valley, even more spectacular in early summer when the gorse is in flower, to Ros Castle on the horizon, the highest point on this part of the fell sandstone ridge. On the left across the Carey Burn, are the scree-covered slopes of Hart Heugh and on its right flank you should be able to see the roughly rectangular shape of a Romano-British settlement.

Continue downhill on the track, past the farm shed and onto the road. Turn left and return to the parking place.

6

Langlee – Old Middleton – Happy Valley. 7km (4½ miles): ascent 190m (623 feet); about 3 hours

A walk along a quiet valley road, then a steep climb up to a good track followed by fairly easy gradients. Good underfoot in all but the worst weathers. Classic Cheviot Hills views on this lovely route which also passes through one of the largest concentrations of ancient British settlements in Northumberland.

The starting place is about 4km (2½ miles) south west of Wooler. To get there, leave Wooler by Cheviot Street. Follow the signs to Earle and Middleton Hall then turn right for Langleeford. Park on the wide grass verge on the right just before Carey Burn Bridge the first bridge in the valley (GR 976250). Set off up the valley road, pausing briefly on the bridge.

The bridge was built in 1956. Prior to this a wooden bridge called Black Bridge and a stone footbridge existed on this spot. Both were washed away in the 1948 floods, but you can still see remains of the abutments of the stone bridge in the banks of the Carey Burn.

Walk on, either on the road or on the haughland beside the Harthope Burn.

The Harthope is one of the prettiest of the Cheviot valleys, particularly in autumn when bracken, the dominant vegetation on the hillsides, turns russet and gold. The valley has always attracted visitors, most notably the eminent 18th century writers Sir Walter Scott and Daniel Defoe. Since then, the invention of the car has made the valley more accessible. To cater for today's visitors, the National Park has reached an access agreement with all the landowners in the Harthope allowing parking and quiet outdoor activities to take place on the flat, grassy areas alongside the burn.

Continue on.

The large coniferous plantation to the right of the road is known as Coronation Wood.

Planted in 1953 to mark the coronation of Queen Elizabeth II, the ripe cones attract flocks of seed-eating siskin.

Cuckoos are also seen around here in spring picking up hairy foxmoth caterpillars, their main source of food, from the dry valley sides. The caterpillars' hairs are irritating enough to deter most enemies except cuckoos, which are either insensitive or too greedy to care.

Carry on along the road and over a cattle grid.

From the higher reaches just below Cheviot, the Harthope Burn traces a fault line in the underlying rock and runs straight and true to Skirl Naked. The burn is fringed by alder woodland. The distinguishing feature of the alder, the main tree in the valley, is the tiny, false cones near the tips of the branches. Green in summer, the cones turn brown and hard in winter. By January they begin to open, releasing seeds each of which has a buoyancy aid on either side.

Alder leaves

Because the trees grow close to water, regeneration is geared to the river system. The seeds fall into the water, float downstream and are cast up onto the gravel beds produced when the burn is in spate. They eventually take root and this is how an even-age stand of alder-carr woodland is formed.

At a point just past the cottage seen to the left, cross the stile by the finger-post signed Middleton Old Town. Go over the bridge across the burn, pass in front of the garden at Langlee Cottage and follow the path uphill. Pause for breath and look back.

Langlee at the foot of the hill was, until recently, a shepherd's cottage. The name means 'a long clearing'. At the head of the valley are the two highest hills in Northumberland, Cheviot 815m (2700 feet) on the right, Hedgehope 714m (2343 feet) on the left.

At the top of the hill the path widens out to a grassy track.

On a clear day, the view straight ahead towards the coast is superb. Cheswick Bay, just south of Berwick can be seen in the gap between the distinctive landmarks of Fenton House (painted white) and the woods on Kyloe Hill.

Walk on. Cross a farm track and head uphill towards the gate on the skyline. Go over the stile by the gate.

The steep-sided little valley on the right is an excellent example of a meltwater channel. This strange feature known as a 'hanging valley' was formed towards the end of the last Ice Age by the abrasive action of water-borne pebbles beneath the underlying surface of the melting glacier.

Wheatear

The sandy sides of the valley, scarred by generations of rabbits using regular runs, provide ideal conditions for a large warren. In summer, wheatears occasionally use the burrows for nesting sites. Sometimes they pay flying visits to these underground chambers, seeking out the juicy insects which live on rabbit droppings.

Keeping the hanging valley on your right, follow the track over the brow of the hill. Cross another track and go down to the fence. Cross over the ladder stile (left of the sheep pens) and walk downhill for about 400m to the right-hand bend in the track.

Langlee Cottage

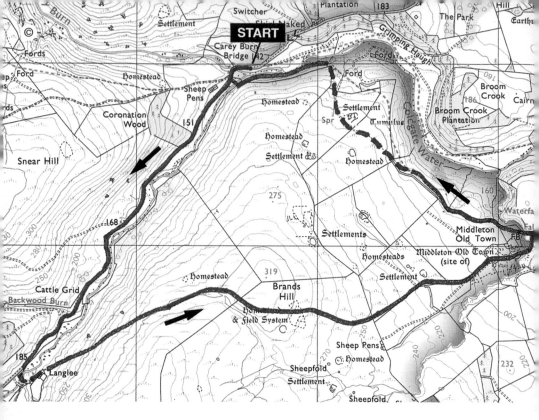

About 10m to the left are the remains of a Romano-British farming settlement occupied during the Roman period. An oval-shaped bank around the settlement encloses house sites on the higher land at the back and a sunken yard at the front where sheep and cattle were kept at night.

Continue on the track to cross another stile by a wall.

The drystone wall on the left has been rebuilt with grant-aid under the National Park's Upland Management Scheme. Rebuilding the ruinous wall presented quite a challenge for the masons who found the walling material extremely difficult to work with. The rounded boulders which make up this wall are all igneous rocks – lavas and granites of the volcanic Cheviot Hills – shaped by water and ice. Drystone walls elsewhere in the county are mainly built of local sandstone, a sedimentary rock which can be split more easily into roughly rectangular blocks.

Walk on, cross another ladder stile and pass in front of the deserted shepherd's cottage.

To the right, on a slight rise, are the remains of several buildings. This was Middleton Old Town, a tiny hamlet which stood here for more than 800 years. The cottages and the corn mill have long since gone but, as you cross the small burn, traces of the mill race can best be seen part way up the slope to the right.

Climb up the track and near the top turn left and go over the footbridge. Bear half right up the bank and head diagonally across the field to the stile in the corner. Cross the stile, follow the path alongside the forest plantation and out over the next stile onto the hillside above Happy Valley.

Happy Valley – a lovely name for a lovely place – so called because in the 19th century, families from the Wooler area came here in summer to picnic and play. Most of the trees in the valley were planted by Austin Kirkup, who owned the Middleton Hall Estate. He won many awards for the design and species mix of his woodlands which he planted over a period of 40 years. He died in 1991 but the plantations are a living reminder of his achievements and of his love of trees in the landscape.

The Harthope Valley

Continue on, keeping the old hedgeline on your left. At the end of the hedgeline, turn left and walk uphill on the track, turning right at the waymarker just as the ground levels out. Follow the wide grass track along the ridge.

On this broad, grassy ridge to the left and right of the track are the homesteads, settlements and field systems of a farming community who wrested a living from this land 2000 years ago. There are more than a dozen of these Romano-British sites on Brand's Hill; several have additional houses built outside the original enclosure a fact which suggests expansion of settlement and population in the uplands of Northumberland at this time.

Carry on downhill on the waymarked track. Go through the gate and immediately bear left onto a path which soon crosses a burn. Continue on to the bottom of the hill where the path meets a fence corner on your left, turn left to walk along the valley side.

This last section of the walk passes through oak and hazel woodland. Hazel can be recognised by the many stems which spring away from ground level. The nuts, green and unripe formed in July, are an important source of food for squirrels. Evidence of their presence can be spotted by the large numbers of split shells scattered about on the woodland floor.

The oak woodland here is believed to be one of the oldest in the area, judging from the diameter of some of the trunks. The trees are rich in insect life and attract a variety of birds including the great spotted woodpecker; its distinctive call can often be heard in the valley in early spring. Green woodpecker is also commonly heard but easily distinguished by its loud highpitched laughing call often described as "yaffling".

After descending the steps, cross the footbridge, then a stile. Turn right onto the road and return to your car.

Hartside – Alnhammoor – Little Dod – Low Bleakhope. 11.5km (7½ miles); ascent 290m (952 feet); about 4½ hours

A good trek into the wild and lonely hill country of the Upper Breamish Valley with breathtaking views all the way. The route passes within sight of two medieval settlements, joins the ancient Salters' Road to Low Bleakhope and returns on a single track tarmac road, following the River Breamish downstream to Hartside.

Although the walk is long and well off the beaten track, it is not particularly strenuous. There are two uphill sections, one on a broad track, the other on the tarmac road. Apart from the odd boggy patches, conditions underfoot are firm.

The starting place is about 10km (6 miles) west of the A697 Powburn to Wooler road. Leave the A697 at the junction signed Ingram, 2km north of Powburn, and follow the road up the valley to Hartside. Park before Hartside Farm, on the grass verge on the left-hand side of the road just before the junction with the private road to Alnhammoor (GR 977162).

Hartside farmhouse was built for W.J.Joicey of Linhope about 1905. The farm buildings are early 19th century although the foundations are reputedly even earlier. The walls and those of the adjoining hayfield are built with the pink and grey igneous rocks which form the Cheviot Hills. These rocks were laid down some 380 million years ago when the whole of this area was an inferno of volcanic activity. The rocks are very hard and almost impossible to split, so wall builders have to rely on loose boulders smoothed and rounded by ice and water. Even these present difficulties for their shape makes them awkward to bed securely. For this reason field walls in the Cheviots are more prone to collapse than those built of fell sandstone which is angular and relatively easy to work. The walls are an integral part of the upland landscape and because it is a constant struggle for the farmer to keep them in good repair, the National Park grant-aids their maintenance in preference to having them replaced with cheaper and less attractive post and wire fencing.

Walk to the junction and turn left along the road signed Alnhammoor. Follow the road round and down as it skirts Hartside Hill on the left.

Hart is the old word for red deer stag. Red deer were once numerous in these hills and valleys when the landscape was more wooded than it is now. The deer have vanished but other wild creatures make their home here, among them the kestrel. It often hovers above the hillside looking for voles, its chief prey, although it will take beetles and insects and in winter, worms. When the kestrel roosts it usually sits on top of the telegraph poles by the roadside, but it is always ready for a snack spotted from its high vantage point.

Cross the bridge over the River Breamish and carry on uphill to the farm.

Swallow

The shepherd's cottage is Alnhammoor. The outbuildings provide nesting sites for a familiar summer visitor, the swallow. After spending the winter in South Africa, the adult birds frequently return to the same place as in previous years, even to the very nests where themselves were hatched. Swallows build their nests of straw, hay and mud collected from puddles and wedged onto rafters in open buildings. They usually raise two broods of four or five young. By August it is possible to judge the success rate when fledglings join their parents in a mass gathering on the overhead wires.

Continue on the road, past the barn and over the cattle grid. Just after the next building leave the road and cross the ladder stile in the wall on the left. Bear half-right to cross another ladder stile in the fence ahead.

Over to the left, below the cottage and close to the confluence of the River Breamish and its tributary the Shank Burn, are the grass-covered remains of several small rectangular buildings. This is the site of Alnhammoor Village, occupied in medieval times and deserted sometime in the 16th century when either hardship or raids by reivers (robbers) from across the Scottish Border forced the population to leave.

At the gate bear right and keeping the Shank Burn on your left follow the path as it goes slightly left downhill to a ladder stile in the fence ahead. Go over the stile and on downhill. Cross the sleeper bridge, bear left and continue alongside the Shank Burn.

The large areas of bare earth on the bankside to the right are the result of rabbits digging. The loose soil provides an ideal seedbed for foxgloves which rabbits don't eat. Rabbits spend most of their day underground or in dense cover. They feed mainly at dusk, night and early morning. With extremely good hearing, all round vision and the ability to spot movement at a long distance they are difficult to get close to – but stoats manage it!

Rabbits

Follow the path as it gradually climbs away from the Shank Burn to the gap in the low bank which crosses the route at right angles.

This bank marks one side of a large, roughly rectangular field associated with another

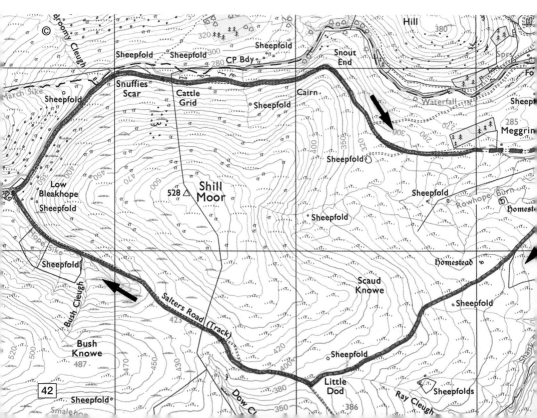

deserted medieval village, Alnhamsheles, located on both sides of the Rowhope Burn. Excavations in the late 1970s – early 1980s showed that the houses were built to a particular style which still persists in parts of the uplands. They were longhouses, with the living room at one end and the byre at the other. The thick walls were faced with large boulders; the hearth consisted of large stones set in a shallow hollow in the floor. In some instances the stone houses had been preceded by timber houses; in two cases there was evidence that the buildings had been destroyed by fire. Pottery from the site suggested that the village was occupied from about 1200 to the 16th century, a fact borne out by documentary records.

Go through the gap and carry straight on uphill for about 250m. Cross another low bank, turn half-left and make for the gate in the fence on the skyline ahead.

From the gate, looking back and to the left, the rounded dome of Hedgehope 714m (2343 feet) second highest hill in the Cheviot range, provides the backdrop to Great and Little Standrop.

Hogdon Law

River Breamish near Alnhammoor

To their right, in the foreground is Ritto Hill near Linhope and beyond Ritto, Long Crag with its rock outcrops.

Go through the gate. Keep straight on a little way, over peaty ground, to join a broad green track for the long ascent up the side of Scaud Knowe. At the highest point on the track turn and look back at the view down the valley.

On the skyline in the far distance is the distinctive hump of Ros Castle, the hill which overlooks Chillingham Park home of the rare, wild white cattle.

As the track bears right to the summit go left onto a path. Follow the contour round Scaud Knowe to meet a broad track at a waymarked junction of tracks.

The ridge on the skyline ahead is broken by the tops of conifers growing in Kidland Forest in Upper Coquetdale. The high hill to the right of the conifers is Cushat Law and to the left, Hogdon Law. In the valley down to the left is a scatter of sheds used for storing hay to feed sheep which winter out on the hills. At the junction turn right. Follow the track uphill and over the ridge to the gate. This track is now a bridleway but it still goes by its old name, the

Salters' Road or 'Theves Rode'. It was named after 18th century traders who smuggled salt by packhorse from salt pans on the North Northumberland coast to Scotland, to avoid paying tax.

Cross the stile by the gate. The way is indistinct here, but keep straight on over rough ground to regain the track as it descends into the valley ahead.

There is considerable evidence of erosion in this long, narrow valley. At one time the Salters' Road ran down Hope Sike at a lower level; the route can still be seen in places, but as ice and rain have taken their toll over the years loosening the soil, the road has collapsed and a new track has been gouged out higher up the hillside. This track too is now being eroded.

Part of the way down the valley on the left, is a small, neatly-built sheep stell with the remains of a stone wall running up to it on both sides. The stell is fairly modern but the fact that it has been built of stone taken from the wall shows how farmers make use of whatever material there is to hand, to provide shelter for sheep in these wild hills.

The farms of High and Low Bleakhope (the nearer of the two), which come into view are among the most isolated settlements in Northumberland. They are 20km from a classified road and 4km from their nearest neighbour, the shepherd at Alnhammoor. In winter even with four-wheel-drive vehicles the access road can be extremely hazardous in snowy or icy conditions.

At the foot of the Hope Sike cross the burn, go past Low Bleakhope then leave the Salters' Road which continues left to High Bleakhope. Turn right onto the tarmac road and carry on as it leads uphill past Snuffies Scar on the right and on across Snout End.

The steady climb is rewarded by dramatic views into the Breamish gorge on the left with the backdrop of Comb Fell, Hedgehope and Dunmoor. On the far hillside is an old rectangular wood, mainly of birch which once would have covered much of the lower slopes in the valley. In prehistoric times a carpet of birch brushwood was laid on top of poles of elm and oak to make trackways across peat bogs. Birch was also used in a more sinister fashion. Chance discoveries of the bodies of prehistoric people in peat bogs have shown that some were strangled and pinned down by birchwood stakes – victims of ritual sacrifice.

Continue along the road, past Ritto Hill and Linhope in the trees to the left, on down to Alnhammoor and back to Hartside.

On the Salters' Road

Ingram – Reaveley Hill – Greensidehill.
10km (6½ miles); ascent 180m (590 feet); about 4½ hours

Good visibility is needed for this walk as part of the way is across bleak terrain. It's a walk of great contrasts between ancient and modern hill farming and between high, open moorland and riverside haughs in the valley below.

Much of the route is over hill pasture, short in places, rough and wet in others. A pleasant meander on grassland by the river between two stretches on a little-used tarmac road, provides welcome relief for tired feet on the return journey.

The starting place is about 5km (3 miles) west of the A697 Powburn to Wooler road. Leave the road at the junction signed Ingram, 2km north of Powburn. Park at Ingram Bridge car park (GR 018163). Turn right out of the car park and cross the bridge.

The haughs and banks of the River Breamish support a thick cover of gorse and broom; in late spring the valley positively glows with the brilliance of their yellow flowers. The prevalence of gorse and broom is the result of seasonal floods. Deposits of sand and gravel brought down by the river are the ideal medium for successful germination and growth of the seeds of these two attractive members of the pea family.

Follow the tarmac road to the first junction on the left.

The stone-faced earth bank on the left is an old field boundary. In the past it was customary to plant banks like this with individual trees and hawthorn hedging. With the passage of time most of the hedging and trees have died. To retain this feature the National Park, in agreement with the landowner, has planted replacement trees in enclosures designed to stop them being eaten by sheep and cattle.

St. Michael's Church

Turn left up the minor road.

The tree stumps behind the fenceline on the left are the sad remains of elms that once lined the roadside. The trees were felled after they succumbed to Dutch elm disease. To the right of the road beyond the rich pastures of Reaveley Farm is Heddon Hill. The parallel lines of earthworks running across the face of the hill are thought to be cultivation terraces dating back to Anglian times before the Norman Conquest. Faced with a shortage of well-drained flat land, people went to considerable effort digging into the hillside to create level areas on which to grow crops of barley and oats.

Go past the junction to Reaveley Farm on the right. After about 90m turn left through the field gate by the fingerpost signed Threestoneburn House. Bear right for a little way, then uphill on the track keeping the fence on your left. Go through the next gate and continue to the ladder stile over the wall at the top of the hill. Turn to look back at the view.

To the left there are distant views down the valley to Ros Castle, the prominent hill on the skyline and further right beyond Old Fawdon Hill in the middle distance, the heather moors near Alnwick.

Below, on the valley floor is Ingram, a small hamlet clustered round the church of St. Michael. Ingram is built just where the River Breamish emerges from the narrow steep-sided upper valley that gives access deep into the border hills. Situated as it is so close to the Border, Ingram was a frequent target for Scots and robber gangs who terrorised the district for hundreds of years. Ingram was provided with a tower for defence against these violent incursions; in 1514 it held a garrison of 40 men. The building which stood close to the river has disappeared, its structure gradually undermined by floodwater. The church with its sturdy, thick-walled tower is the only reminder now of more turbulent times in the history of the Breamish Valley.

Climb the stile over the wall and follow the grassy track as it heads on uphill to the derelict house of Reaveleyhill.

Reaveleyhill used to be a shepherd's cottage but it has lain empty for many years. Its demise is symptomatic of the changes that have taken place in hill farming since the Second World War. Today shepherding of large, remote areas in the uplands is often carried out from the main farm, using tractors and ATVs (All Terrain Vehicles), so there is no need for a shepherd to live in an isolated steading to keep a watchful eye on his flock. The increased mobility of farmers has also resulted in a decline in the number of shepherds employed in hill farming. Abandoned by humans, Reaveleyhill is now home to pigeons and swallows.

Pass the front of the cottage and continue on the grassy track keeping parallel to the fence over to the right. Cross a narrow burn and at the top of the next rise go straight on, passing any tracks off to the left.

The view opens out to the border hills. Looking ahead, past the corner of Threestoneburn plantation, are Cunyan Crags with Dunmoor Hill behind and slightly to their right, the conical top of Hedgehope Hill.

The Cheviot grasslands provide an extensive wildlife habitat but the variety of creatures found here is relatively poor. The birds you are most likely to see on these high windswept hills are summer visitors – lapwing, curlew,

Reaveleyhill

meadow pipit and skylark – which come to breed. Foxes make their home among the rocks or secluded bracken beds, and some are still bold enough to be seen hunting.

Keep to the track as it bears left around the hillside until a small stone-built cairn on a hillock appears about 45m to the left. At this point leave the track and bear right downhill in the direction of the black hayhut and walled enclosure on the hillslope opposite.

The walled enclosure was one of the gathering places used by hill shepherds in times past. They met here about twice a year to return to their owners sheep that had strayed.

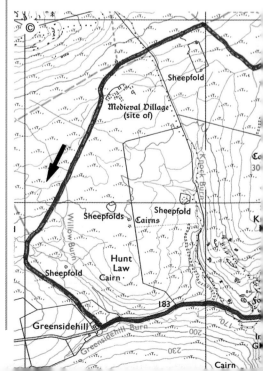

Meadow pipit

covered wall footings of at least 15 rectangular stone houses and yards with associated field walls. A large area of rig and furrow on the more gently sloping land below the village, together with stone clearance piles and a possible corn-drying kiln suggest that the villagers were able to grow cereal crops – oats and barley – on this sheltered site in the hills. Why they abandoned the settlement is unrecorded, perhaps frequent destruction by Scottish raids or a change to colder, wetter conditions making it impossible to cultivate crops successfully. The actual reason will probably never be known.

The path is ill-defined but go left along the top of the bank above the little burn then downhill over a sleeper bridge and on to meet a grassy track. Bear right uphill on the track. Leave the track where it bears left towards the hayhut and continue on a faint path for about 100m to a four-way way-marker post. Turn left and follow the sheep track straight on to the gate in the fence. Go through the gate and after about 180m the path passes close to the site of a medieval village.

The remains on the ground show that this has been a substantial settlement. There are grass-

Bear slightly left and continue over wet, rough, almost featureless pasture to a drain-age ditch. Cross this and turn right. Follow the ditch downhill and recross it further on. Keep straight on along the line of an earth bank and another drainage ditch. After about 270m cross a sleeper bridge over the bank and ditch. Carry on in the direction of the left-hand plantation seen ahead. Go over two burns then bear left along the hill-side above the sheep stell, below left. Make for the left-hand end of the wall ahead. Go through the wicket gate in the fence to the left of the field gate in the wall.

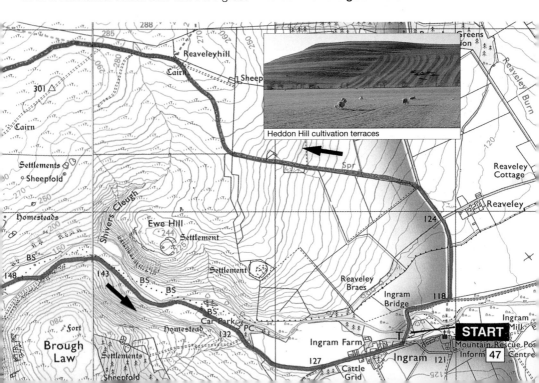
Heddon Hill cultivation terraces

In the field over the wall to the right is a series of chestnut paling fencing. This is a snow baffle, put up to prevent snow drifting in and blocking the road to Hartside and other farms higher up the valley.

Continue down to Greensidehill, passing to the left of the farmhouse. Go through the wicket gate next to the fingerpost and turn left along the road to reach the bridge over the river in about 1.5km.

The scree-covered slopes of Brough Law, the steep-sided hill ahead and to the right of the road, is Ingram Glidders (loose stones). Scree was formed about 18,000 years ago when huge ice sheets blanketed the north. From time to time temperatures improved but the process of alternately thawing then freezing again shattered the rocks. As a result the surface of steep hills became covered with an unstable layer of stone fragments – scree. Such places are unsafe for walkers, even sheep pick their way with care.

On top of Brough Law is a prehistoric hillfort with a massive stone rampart, part of which is visible from the road. It is accessible from the car park at Bulby's Wood about 1.5km further down the valley. Legend has it that a local huntsman, Black Tom, was pursued across Brough Law by the terrible Shadow on the Moor. He and his horse plunged over the Glidders to their deaths in the river below.

Cross the bridge.

The bridge is known locally as Peggy Bell's Bridge. Before the bridge was built in 1910 the only way across the river at this point was by the ford which was impassable after heavy rain. The popular story is that after floodwater prevented the Adamson family who lived at Linhope from getting to Doncaster for the St. Ledger, they provided the money for a bridge. The bridge was named after Peggy Bell, the shepherd's daughter from Greensidehill who used the bridge to get to school at Ingram. The school is now the National Park Centre.

The green track at the foot of The Glidders is the only visible sign of the track bed of a light railway which transported stone from the scree to rebuild sections of washed-out road in the valley.

Leave the road and continue along the haughland beside the river on the left for about 1.5km to the car park at Bulby's Wood.

An obvious bird along this stretch of the valley in summer is the cuckoo. It winters in North Africa but comes to this country to breed; the summer sun is less blistering here and there are lots of insects for hungry nestlings to eat. The male arrives in mid-May in the uplands and sits about on the top of hawthorns or telegraph wires calling 'cuckoo' to attract a female. She lays a single egg in each of a number of meadow pipits' nests and removes one of the eggs. When the young cuckoo hatches it murders the rightful inhabitants and takes the food brought by the poor pipit foster parents.

The haughland along the river has always been popular with visitors. Although the land belongs to the Northumberland Estates, a Management Agreement between the landowner, the tenant farmer and the National Park allows picnicking and other outdoor activities on this lovely stretch of riverside.

At Bulby's Wood, leave the haughland, walk along the road, past the fields and sheds of Ingram Farm and back to the car park at Ingram Bridge.

Scree slopes above River Breamish

Ingram – Wether Hill – Cochrane Pike – Fawdon.
8km (5 miles); ascent 260m (853 feet); about 2½ – 3 hours

A pleasant hill walk in a lovely part of Northumberland with good views over the Breamish Valley. Apart from one steep climb, the uphill sections are all fairly gentle. The outward route follows the old track between Ingram and Prendwick; the return is on a good footpath and then another track. Conditions underfoot are generally firm.

The starting place is about 5km (3 miles) west of the A697 Powburn to Wooler road. Leave the road at the junction signed Ingram, 2km north of Powburn. Park at Ingram Bridge car park (GR 018163). Walk along the road past the telephone box to the junction. Turn left and continue on until you reach the fingerpost signed Prendwick on the right.

The building just ahead is Ingram Parish Hall. It was built with money left over from the fund raised to commemorate local people killed in the First World War. Most of the fund had been used to build the lychgate by the church; the residue of £500 was sufficient to cover the expense of a hall.

The hall was opened in 1929. Running costs included three farthings an hour for heating by a woodburning stove and half a penny an hour for gas lighting. Dances were held to raise money to pay the bills and to buy a piano. The Parish Hall Minute Book records that the Chairman of the Hall Committee, the Rev. R.F. Allgood, "was authorised to get someone who understood pianos to choose one up to the value of £25".

Go through the field gate by the fingerpost. Keeping the fence on your left walk uphill to the stile. Cross over, turn right along the track and continue to the gate.

Grassy terraces can be seen on nearby hill-sides, the work of medieval or later ploughmen.

When the field is on a slope constant ploughing will cause some of the earth from the top to slip down to the bottom and form a bank; this is known as a lynchet. In medieval times, villagers would have had small cultivated fields running across the hillsides and separated by strips of unploughed land.

Go through the gate, keep on, over another stile by a gate and follow the track which climbs gently for about 800m.

On the summit of Wether Hill to the right is one of the best examples of an Iron Age hillfort in Northumberland. Inside the double rampart which encloses the settlement are the circular foundations of about 20 tightly-packed timber houses.

At the fork go left, across a wet area and carry on downhill on the track.

On a clear day the Simonside Hills south of Rothbury come into view and nearer to hand the hamlet of Prendwick lies half hidden in the trees. Peaceful as it is today and seemingly far from Scotland, in the times of the Border Troubles from the late 13th-early 17th centuries, this area was ever on the alert. There were six men on watch from "Prendeke to Engram" to give warning should the Scottish reivers be seen riding over the hills to "do a little shifting"(stealing).

About 120m before the gate leading to the enclosed field, turn left at the waymarker and continue down the sunken path to the wicket gate.

This gate is a hunt wicket in the boundary fence between two farms. It allows hunt followers on horseback access from one farm to another. Three packs of foxhounds hunt the Cheviot Hills, The College Valley, The West Percy and The Border.

Fox cub

Go through the gate and left uphill on an obvious path. At the top of the steep bracken-covered slope bear right. Follow the edge of the bracken down towards a fence ahead. About 100m before the fence, turn left along the path which gradually leads away from the fence on your right towards the plantation and shed below Old Fawdon Hill on the left.

Brown hares live in open countryside and these hillsides are an ideal habitat for them. They live above ground in well-defined territories spending the day lying in shallow depressions, under cover. Hares are larger than their relative the rabbit. They have longer ears and longer hind legs, their colour is a mixture of brown-grey hairs and the ears have black tips. Hares feed mainly in the twilight, on grass, roots or young trees. The mad March hares are the males which bound, kick and stand on their hind legs to box each other in a ritual that impresses the female before mating.

Pass just to the right of the trees and the shed.

This has been a marshy area so the dampish soil is the place to find 'cuckoo flower', also called lady's-smock. The flower appears with the cuckoo in early summer and may be white or lilac in colour. Some of the leaves form a

Lady's-smock

rosette on the ground, but the ones on the stem are ladder-like. The orange tip butterfly lays its eggs on lady's smock. The female, searching for the correct plant which will eventually feed her caterpillars, drums on the leaves with her front pair of feet. This releases scent from the leaf surface, and in the butterfly the sense of taste is apparently conveyed from the feet to the brain, so the insect can judge whether or not the plant on which it has settled is the correct one to nurture its caterpillars. The butterfly flits from flower to flower, laying an egg here and there on the flower stalk or base of a bud. In this way the caterpillars are spread out; they are cannibalistic and would eat each other if they were crowded together.

View north west over Ingram and Breamish Valley

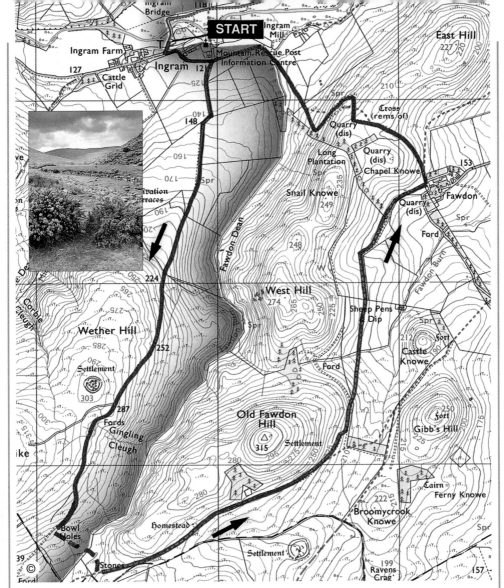

Walk down the track at the bottom of the steep hillside and continue on, keeping left and above another plantation on the right. Follow the fence line on the right until you come to a gate and a stile.

On the slope away to the right is another prehistoric settlement; the ramparts and ditches can be clearly seen. There are many of these scattered about the lower hillsides, some dating from the Bronze Age, around 3,500 years ago, and some dating from the time the Romans were in Britain. The economy of these settlements was essentially that of farmer and herdsman.

Cross the stile and walk diagonally left across the field to the gate. Go through the gate and straight on towards a hedge uphill of the sheep pens on the right. Two sets of gates are reached. Go through the left-hand one and follow the path beside the hedge on the right.

Everyone knows the old saying "Cast not a clout till May be out". In many country districts hawthorn is still called "May" from the time of year when the tree flowers. Another name for hawthorn is quickthorn, so called because it grows very quickly. When it is properly layered it makes a dense, prickly hedge which is a deterrent to man and beast but a good nesting site for small songbirds.

Apart from its use in celebrations connected with the coming of summer, hawthorn has other more strange associations as for instance with the mysterious Green Man A pagan symbol of man's unity with the natural world who was later absorbed into the Christian tradition, he appears in folklore, mythology, religion, art and architecture throughout Europe, often wearing a wreath of hawthorn on his head.

The Green Man .

Continue on below a line of trees to the left. Go through the gate, carry on to the cottage at Fawdon. Go through another gate, turn left and head uphill towards the trees. Follow the track which zigzags downhill to the next gate.

In 1587, 500 Border Reivers, mostly from the Armstrong clan rode down from Scotland and raided Ryle, Prendwick and Ingram. They took 500 cattle, 300 sheep and 20 prisoners. The raid was one of many inflicted on the district over a period of 400 years.

The route down affords excellent views up the Breamish Valley. Hedgehope 714m (2343 feet), the second highest hill in Northumberland, is seen ahead. Brough Law, encircled by the walls of an Iron Age hillfort, rises above the plantation to the left of the River Breamish.

West Hill

Continue on the track across the field and turn left onto the road. Follow the road on and go through the gate.

Down to the right is the National Park Centre at Ingram, formerly the village school. Opposite is St. Michael's Church, dating from the 11th century. Like many early country churches in Northumberland it went through a period of neglect before being restored in the mid-19th century. Even the sturdy medieval tower was taken down and rebuilt stone by stone. Despite all this renovation the interior still manages to retain the atmosphere of a very old and unspoilt little church.

At the road junction keep straight on and retrace your steps to the car park.

The Yett on the Moor

Alnham – White Gate – Hazeltonrig. 7.5km (5 miles); ascent 210m (689 feet); about 3 hours

Starting on the outskirts of Alnham, the walk follows an uphill route with excellent views south over the fertile vale of Whittingham to the Simonside Hills beyond, and north to the foothills of The Cheviot. The steeper parts are not too taxing; the rest of the way is over gently undulating ground with several small upland burns to cross. Route finding is easy; there are good tracks and paths. In wet weather however, the initial uphill section can be boggy.

Park on the grass verge close to the wall by Alnham Church (GR 991109). Set off along the road, past the church and the former vicarage with its adjoining peel tower.
The church and peel are visible reminders of Alnham's long and sometimes turbulent history. Dedicated to St. Michael and All Angels, the church dates back to the 12th century. It was extensively restored in 1870 after ravages of time and rural depopulation led to its neglect. A surveyor's report of 1862 gives a graphic account of the state of the building:

> 'the eye is met by damp, mildewed walls, and by streaks of sky seen through the unceiled slates. . . the window sashes let in wind and rain. . . three of the worm-eaten, mousy pews are square. . . fungi abound, and the pavement is sodden with damp. Ruin is imminent. . . '

The restored vicar's peel, now a private house and reputedly haunted, is mentioned in Henry VIII's Border Survey, 1541. Fortified buildings such as this were a necessity of life in those days. The ground floor was used for storage; the occupants lived upstairs where they would be safer in the event of an attack by the infamous Border Reivers. At one stage the Earl of Northumberland wrote to the king

> 'The Scottes. . . . brunte a towne of mine called Alenam. . . . with all the corne, hay and householde stuf and also a woman.'

Turn right before the cattle grid and follow the track signed Salters' Road beside the vicarage garden wall. Go through the gate and on uphill beside the wall on the left to another gate. Go through this gate, continue alongside a conifer wood on the right and through another gate into a narrow fenced area next to a mixed woodland.
This woodland was established in 1905 and unusually for that time in an upland area, it was planted with a variety of tree species – Scots pine, larch, rowan, oak, ash and sycamore. Holes in the trunks of some of the older trees make good nesting sites for birds, notably the great spotted woodpecker. Puncture holes on the underside of dead branches which have had their bark stripped off are a sure sign of woodpecker activity. Its alarm call is a hard, metallic 'chink' repeated at intervals.

Continue uphill to the gate in the fence ahead. Go through the gate and bear right beside a small burn to reach the track on the skyline in about 200m. At the track, turn and look at the view over Whittingham Vale.
Whittingham Vale is a district in the upper reaches of the River Aln. The river has its source in the hills above Alnham and flows eastwards past the town of Alnwick to empty its waters in the North Sea at Alnmouth. The high ridge to the south – Thrunton Woods and Long Crag slightly left, Simonside to the right – forms the barrier between the Vale of Whittingham and Coquetdale beyond.

The Simonside Hills from Salters' Road

Follow the track to the top of the hill. As the track bears right walk straight on along a sunken grassy track descending gradually to the Coppath Burn.

This track is part of the long distance cross-country route known as the Salters' Road described in Walk 7.

The wet, rushy areas on the edge of the Coppath Burn are a perfect hiding place for snipe, a small wading bird with a very long bill. With its russet and gold feathers, fringed with white, it is well camouflaged and will remain unnoticed until almost underfoot. Only then will it suddenly take off, startling the unsuspecting walker with its alarm call 'snipe-snipe' and flying erratically until it is out of sight.

Keep to the track as it crosses the burn and bears left towards the field wall ahead. Make for the gate.

This is the White Gate. A gate or 'yett' was an opening or entrance to another area, in this case, the entrance to the summer grazing grounds. 'White' probably referred to the moor mat-grass which dies back in winter and is bleached by the weather. Sheep don't particularly like mat-grass because it is rough and unpalatable, but what may be distasteful to one creature is manna from heaven to another. Moorland mat-grass is the main food plant of the larvae of the antler moth. The adult moth gets its name from the distinctive antler-shaped markings on its wings. In warm weather, especially in August and early September, the antler moth can be seen during the day as it visits the flowers of thistles and other plants to feed on the nectar.

Cross the ladder stile by the gate and bear left, walking over rough grassland until the conifer plantation comes into view ahead.

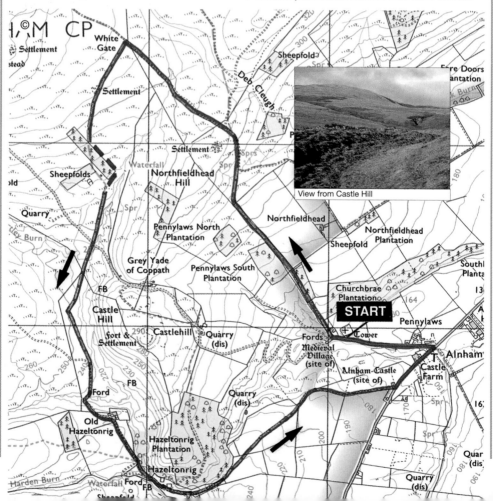

View from Castle Hill

After about 180m you reach a grass-covered earthwork on the right. This is a Romano-British farmstead. It occupies a comparatively sheltered position and although part of the enclosure bank has been destroyed at some time in the past, enough of the settlement survives to show there had been several round houses inside.

Near the settlement join the wide grassy track which leads towards the plantation. Turn left and with the fence on your right walk down to the corner. Turn right and continue on the track with the Coppath Burn down on your left.

The sheep which rake this valley are Cheviots, identifiable by their pricked ears, tight, white fleece, white face and Roman nose. Not as hardy as the Scottish blackface and the Swaledale or their crossbreeds, Cheviots prefer the lower ground where there is more shelter.

Cheviot sheep

Continue on the track to the road.

The red and white poles beside the bridge and alongside the road are snow markers. They are there to indicate the edge of the road when the area is deep in snow. In winter and early spring sudden heavy snowfalls, 'whiteouts' as they

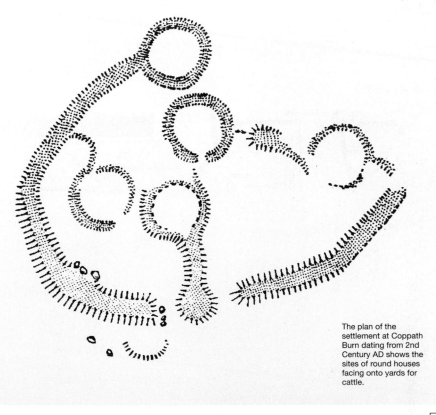

The plan of the settlement at Coppath Burn dating from 2nd Century AD shows the sites of round houses facing onto yards for cattle.

are known, make the surrounding landscape unrecognisable and even those who have lived here all their lives can become disorientated.

Cross the road. Keep straight on across the small footbridge over the Spartley Burn.

The extensive bracken beds round here provide enough cover and food for the wren, a small bird with a very loud voice. Despite the absence of woodland and scrub, it is one of the few birds you are likely to see and hear most of the year in the uplands.

Bear right and walk uphill to the gate ahead. Go through the gate and follow the path, bearing left along the hillside above the burn.

There's a colony of moles living in this area. The pasture is littered with mounds of soil produced when they excavate their burrow system, which provides safe housing, a reservoir for air and a catchment for food. Their staple diet is earthworms, supplemented by any insect larvae, such as leatherjackets, that may fall into the burrows. In wet areas such as this, you may occasionally come across a

Molecatcher's gibbet

huge molehill as much as 1 metre in diameter and 0.5 metre high. This is known as a fortress. At its base is the nest which the mole has to ensure is above the water table, otherwise the young would drown.

Continue on to join a track which leads down to Hazeltonrig Burn. Cross the burn to the right of the farm buildings seen ahead. Walk up the hillslope and just before you reach the gate pause to look back.

On the top of Castle Hill to the right, is a well-defended hillfort, built about 2,500 years ago. Part of the outer rampart can be seen on the skyline. The large number of prehistoric

Ewartly Shank from Whitegate

Alnham Village

hillforts, settlements and burial grounds in the area suggest that this valley was a good place to live in those days. The climate was warmer than it is now so settlement was possible even at this high altitude, 300m (almost 1000 feet) above sea level.

Go through the gate, then left around and in front of the stone buildings of Old Hazeltonrig. Continue on and where the track turns right downhill, walk straight on to the corner of the fence ahead. Go through the wicket gate and, keeping the woodland on your left, continue downhill to rejoin the track.

The close-cropped grassy bank to the left of the track supports a rich variety of plants including lady's mantle, yarrow, bitter vetch, thyme, heather and the lovely little mouse-eared hawkweed with its cinnamon-yellow flowers and spoon-shaped hairy leaves arranged in tiny rosettes.

Cross the footbridge over the Spartley Burn.

The woodland on the left is dominated by beech, easily identified in winter by its smooth, pale grey-green bark and long pointed buds. In autumn the woodland undergoes a transformation as the leaves turn to copper and gold.

Climb the stile and continue on the track past the bungalow, then left on the grassy track which winds uphill to the gate. Go through the gate and, keeping to the track, continue on across improved pasture and through another two gates. After about 100m you reach a fourth gate by the wall end. Go through this gate and follow the track alongside the hedge to another gate which leads you out onto the road. Turn left and continue along the road to the junction.

In summertime to the left of the road there is a huge patch of what looks like rhubarb. The broad, spreading leaves are in fact the leaves of butterbur, a plant which thrives in moist, peaty soil. The leaves are preceded in spring by large candle-like flowers varying in shade from white through to pink. The leaves were once used to wrap butter in, to keep it moist and cool. The root, powdered and taken in wine was believed to be a cure for infections of the bladder and for worms.

At the junction turn left again for Alnham Church.

Just before you reach the church look over the wall to the left of the road. The stretch of water is the old mill pond. It was rescued from dereliction in the mid 1980s by a partnership between the landowner and the National Park who grant-aided its restoration. The pond was re-excavated, the dam and weir repaired and a tree-planting scheme carried out. The work has not only saved a piece of Alnham's historic past for posterity but has created a valuable habitat for all manner of wildlife.

11 Buckham's Bridge – Deel's Hill – Chew Green – Lamb Hill – Yearning Hall – Blindburn. 14.5km (9 miles); ascent 280m (919 feet); about 5 hours

The River Coquet is Northumberland's longest river. From its source in wet ground at Coquethead it gathers strength and momentum on its 88km (55 miles) journey to the North Sea. For the first few miles the Coquet twists through a narrow upland valley fringed with bare domed hills.

This route is on the north side of that valley. It includes a ridge walk to begin with, the option of visiting the remote, Roman staging post of Chew Green near Coquethead; a lengthy stretch following the Pennine Way along the Border fence with outstanding views into Scotland, a chance to traverse an expanse of wild moorland and a gentle descent down the rugged valley of the Blindburn, a tributary of the River Coquet.

The steepest ascent is at the start thereafter there are good level stretches interspersed with rough walking. At certain times of the year and after prolonged wet weather parts of the route may be very boggy. This is a walk for blue sky days. There are clear tracks and paths but wayfinding can be difficult, particularly if the weather turns misty as there are few identifiable features in the landscape.

To reach the start leave the B6341 Rothbury to Elsdon road at Swindon if you are approaching from Elsdon, or Flotterton, from Rothbury. Both junctions are signed Alwinton. Go through Harbottle and on to Alwinton. Go through Alwinton and continue on the narrow single track road up the valley of the River Coquet for about 15km (9½ miles) past Blindburn Farm and park at Buckham's Bridge car park on the right (GR 824107).

From the car park cross the footbridge over Buckham's Walls Burn, go through the field gate and follow the track uphill.

Moles and thistles make a bad combination on this hilltop and judging from the number of molehills there's a lot of underground activity taking place. Fresh soil pushed up by their tunnelling makes an ideal seed bed for spear thistles. The mauve florets in the flowerheads are pollinated by butterflies, bees and insects with long tongues able to reach down to the nectar. The seeds, attached to the base of downy hairs, float off like parachutes in the wind to germinate in another molehill.

Spear Thistle

The leaves and stem of the spear thistle are very spiny and this is the plant's main defence against grazing animals. The spines are also painful to humans. Tradition has it that this was why the thistle was chosen as the emblem of Scotland. Apparently in the 8th century, the Danes tried to capture the stronghold on top of Castle Rock in Stirling. Their scouts approached the base of the rock at nightfall, barefoot and in the darkness failed to see the thistles. Their cries of pain raised the alarm and the attack was repulsed.

Pass the large upstanding stone on the left and go through the gate in the fence ahead.

The grim, furrowed hill on the far side of the valley is Thirl Moor. At the foot of Thirl Moor is Fulhope, the last occupied farm in Upper Coquetdale. Fulhope is first mentioned in written records in 1331 and later variously appears as Fair or Foul Philip. A 'hope' is a sheltered valley and in this wild part of Northumberland perhaps 'foul' meaning 'difficult' is an appropriate description. In 1399 on the hillside above Fulhope, a band of marauding Scots was defeated by an English force under Robert de Umfraville, Lord of Redesdale. He took many prisoners including three Scottish Knights, for this he was made a Knight of the Garter by King Henry IV.

Continue to the fork in the track. Take the left fork signed Deel's Hill on the waymarker.

Deel's is a corruption of 'Devil' but what the implication is, is anyone's guess.

After crossing the top of the hill, the track gradually descends to the saddle where it forks. Take the right fork and keep straight on past another track joining from the left to reach wet ground. Follow the way-marked route across the boggy area then bear left uphill on a clear track. After cresting the hill head towards the four-way fingerpost near the fence which marks the border with Scotland. At this point you have the option of a linear extension by turning left to visit the Roman earthworks at Chew Green (about 1km). If you decide to continue on omit the route directions to Chew Green and back.

ROUTE TO CHEW GREEN

At the fingerpost turn left onto the Pennine Way and follow the track downhill. Cross the stile next to the gate. Walk on for about 180m until you reach a fingerpost where the track bears left. Leave the track and go straight on in the direction signed Chew Green.

The main grass in this area is moor mat-grass (Nardus stricta) with a high proportion of wavy hair-grass, particularly to the left of the track. It has fine leaves and silvery spikelets bearing distinctive, almost heart-shaped seed heads which turn pinkish-red in late July.

Continue down the track to cross the stone bridge over Chew Sike. Climb up out of the burn then bear left downhill. Go over a small sleeper bridge and on across level ground to reach the Roman earthworks on the right.

The Roman military called this place Ad Fines (the End of the World) and indeed it must have seemed like that especially on blustery, rain-soaked days. Even their modern counterparts who come here to train regard this area as Ad Fines. Chew Green was a staging post on the Roman road of Dere Street which runs close by. The Romans chose the site with care. The complex series of earthworks which includes early marching camps and a smaller second century fortlet occupies a reverse slope position. This meant that any attacking force from the north coming over the skyline, would be clearly visible to the Roman sentries below.

On the Pennine Way near Brownhart Law

Wild goats near Hindhope

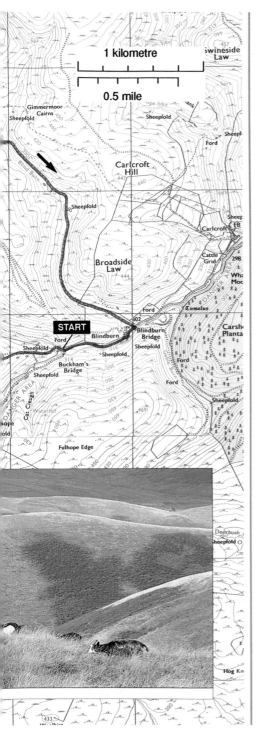

The five-point metal stars at several places around the earthworks are symbols used by the army to indicate sites of archaeological interest which must not be damaged by troops.

Return to the fingerpost beyond Chew Sike.

At the fingerpost head off in the direction signed Lamb Hill. After about 90m cross the stile next to a gate in the fence. Continue on the track round Brownhart Law and back to the starting point of the route to Chew Green.

The track follows the course of Dere Street, the main Roman road running north from York to Inverness. Today much of the route is covered by the A68 but in the 18th century a new road, the A696 from Newcastle to Otterburn was extended through the Upper Rede Valley over Carter Bar and into Scotland, avoiding the difficult cross-country line through the hills taken by the Roman road. After this Dere Street north of the A696 went out of use as a road and has become a scenic route for walkers. This section is part of the Pennine Way. In the heather over the fence are the remains of a small Roman signal station visible as a rectangle outlined by a low bank and ditch. The entrance faces Dere Street. The signal station commands extensive views north and west and was probably a forward observation post for Chew Green.

ROUTE CONTINUED

Continue alongside the Border fence on the left. There is some boggy ground to negotiate along the way.

From here you can see for miles into Southern Scotland. Across Hindhope Farm in the valley below and slightly left over the conifer forests, is the long ridge of Carter Fell on the Border; moving right the conical hill in the far distance is Rubers Law, site of another Roman signal station and right again the valley of the Jed Water with the Tweed Basin beyond.

Anywhere along the next section of the walk from Brownhart Law to the Pennine Way shelter near Lamb Hill, you could well see family groups of wild goats. The Hindhope herd is one of three that forage in the border hills, the others are based on Kielderhead Moor in the North Tyne and in the College Valley near Wooler. The adult billies are fairly easy to recognise, they have huge horns and a heavy growth of shaggy hair round the neck and beard. Wild goats are very shy which is just as well as the billies in particular have a fragrance all of their own. They urinate on the themselves to attract the females – once smelled, never forgotten!

At the next fingerpost Dere Street and the Pennine Way part company. Dere Street goes through the gate onto the north side of the Border fence, the Pennine Way continues on the south side. Keep on the Pennine Way in the direction signed Lamb Hill.

The views across this vast expanse of bleak wilderness are north to the folded foothills of the Cheviots with Cheviot itself prominent in the background.

Dere Street, near the Border Fence

Bear right across undulating ground, wet in places with duckboards over the worst sections. The path is sometimes indistinct but the route is well waymarked. After about 2km the path crosses the steep-sided Rennies Burn. Climb to the waymarker at the corner of the fence, bear left and walk downhill to the small hut seen ahead.

The hut variously called Lamb Hill or Yearning Saddle shelter, was built by National Park staff and volunteers in the late 1970s to provide emergency overnight accommodation and a refuge for Pennine Way walkers on the last stretch of the national trail, through the Cheviot hills. This hut and another at Auchope Cairn on the shoulder of Cheviot, split the final 39km (23 miles) distance from Byrness to Kirk Yetholm into manageable sections, providing safe havens should the weather deteriorate.

From the shelter the Pennine Way continues uphill next to the fence. Your route now leaves the Pennine Way. Turn right and follow the track as it contours around the foot of Lamb Hill. At the highest

point go past the path leading off to the left and continue on the main track downhill. After about 180m and just after a wet, rushy area there is a group of low grassy banks to the right and left of the track.

From this complex of enclosures it is possible to trace the remains of rectangular buildings and cattleyards which suggest that this was a pastoral settlement. The site possibly dates to medieval times but it isn't documented so why it was situated here, how long it was occupied and by whom will probably never be known.

At this point bear left off the track onto a narrow path leading to Yearning Hall.

The dominant plant on this broad plateau is purple moor-grass, often called 'flying bent'. In summer when it is flowering over a wide area the ground appears to be covered in a purple-brown mist. In autumn its broad leaves turn a lovely pale straw colour and in winter they break off and fly about in the strong wind, hence the name 'flying bent'.

The path rises to a little knoll then continues downhill to the derelict building at Yearning Hall.

'Hall' seems a rather grand name for this former shepherd's cottage. Yearning Hall is first mentioned in the 1851 Census and was abandoned about 1940 during the Second World War, when the area north of the River Coquet was used by the Ministry of Defence for live firing.

You can sometimes see wild goats around here; it's fairly sheltered and in late summer there are plenty of nettles and sweet grass for them to eat.

Pass in front of the house and drop down into the steep gully ahead, climb out on the narrow path and with the Yearning Burn on your right contour round the hillside. Go downhill, crossing the Blindburn near its confluence with the Yearning Burn. Keeping the Blindburn on your right continue downstream to the green hayhut on a broad grassy area by the waterside.

Go past the hayhut and around the foot of the hillside on your left towards the sheep stell ahead. Pass right of the stell and carry on down the Blindburn.

Brown trout live in the burn. Spawning occurs in autumn and winter on shallow areas in running water. The female makes a small channel in the gravel, lays her eggs then covers them over by flicking the gravel back with vigorous movements of her tail. The eggs hatch out in one to two months and the young trout (fry) emerge from the gravel in March. Their main food supply at this stage is insect larvae; adult brown trout eat insects, minnows and their own young!

Keep on. Cross two stiles and continue to the sleeper bridge.

The wet flush near the sleeper bridge contains marsh lousewort. The name is derived from the long-held superstition that this purple-flowered plant infected sheep with lice. Marsh lousewort is rare in upland Northumberland possibly because shepherds may have pulled it out in the belief that it is a host of the sheep parasite liver fluke. The plant itself is a semi-parasite, obtaining some of its food from the roots of other neighbouring plants.

Marsh lousewort

Go over the bridge and continue towards Blindburn. Cross three stiles to reach the road. At the road turn right, walk between the farm buildings and return to your car.

Eildon Hills and the Scottish Lowlands from Black Halls

12

The Street – Windy Gyle – Trows Law. 11.5km (7½ miles); ascent 350m (1148 feet); about 4½ hours

A strenuous hill walk in Upper Coquetdale, one of the most dramatic landscapes in the National Park. The outward journey follows an old drovers' route the Street, to Windy Gyle and Russell's Cairn on the Scottish Border. The uphill gradients are long but only the final section to the summit is steep. On a fine day the views in all directions are incomparable.

The going is generally good underfoot but in adverse conditions route finding may be difficult so choose settled weather for this walk.

To reach the start, leave the B6341 Rothbury to Elsdon road at Swindon if you are approaching from Elsdon, or Flotterton, from Rothbury. Both junctions are signed Alwinton. From Harbottle continue on to Alwinton the last hamlet in Upper Coquetdale. Keep on up the valley for another 10km (6 miles). Park on the grass near the bridge at the fork in the road 1km beyond Windyhaugh in Upper Coquetdale (GR 860115).

The parking area is the site of the Slyme Foot pub, the most notorious drinking den in Upper Coquetdale in the late 18th century. Standing at the confluence of the Rowhope Burn and the River Coquet, it was a convenient overnight resting place for Scottish cattle drovers bringing their herds to market in England.

Joined by local shepherds they indulged in an orgy of gambling and drinking, chiefly whisky from several illicit stills which operated in the secluded valleys around here. The key to the pub was reputed to be hidden under the large whinstone rock on the north bank of the burn close to the road bridge.

Cross the bridge, bear right over the stile and climb steeply uphill, keeping the fence on your left.

You are now walking on The Street, an ancient drove road running from Slyme Foot up to the Border and down to the Kale Water in Scotland. On the military map produced in 1755 by General Roy, it was called 'Clattering Path', perhaps a comment on the sound of cattle hooves on the stony ground. Below, to the right, is the valley of the Rowhope Burn and the farm buildings of Rowhope and Trows beyond. The high point at the head of the valley is Windy Gyle, the ultimate destination of the walk.

As the gradient eases cross the stile in the fence on the left. Turn right and continue on to the corner of the fence. Turn right again and, with the fence on your right carry on, passing a stile and gate on the right, to cross the stile by the gate ahead.

Below left is the Coquet Valley. It is hard to believe this is part of a military training area, unless you happen to be walking when low flying or live firing is taking place on the far side of the valley, disturbing the tranquillity of these lonely hills. The Otterburn Training Area is the largest single military training ground in the British Isles. Over 23,472 hectares (58,000 acres) of land in Upper Coquetdale and Upper Redesdale, one fifth of the Northumberland National Park, are owned by the Ministry of Defence. The River Coquet is the boundary between the live firing area to the south and the non-firing area to the north.

Continue on for about 70m. Leave the track and bear right around Hindside Knowe.

Military range warning sign and flag

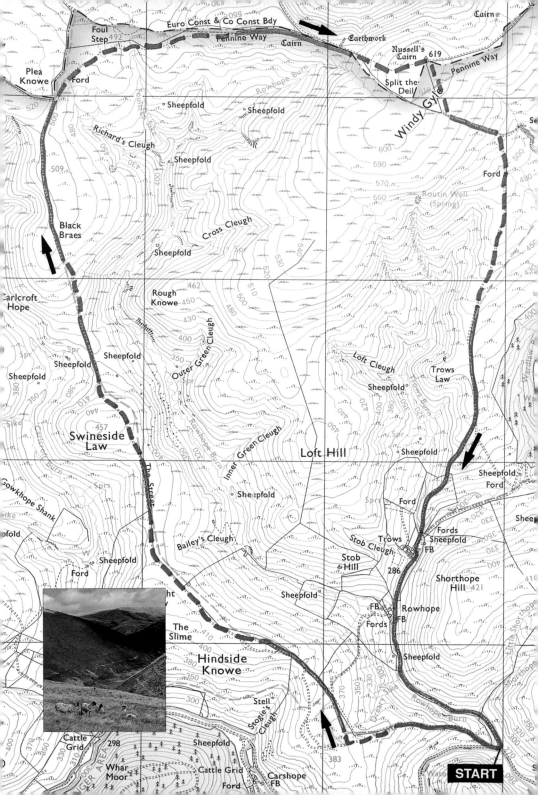

Foul Step 492
Plea Knowe
Ford
Euro Const & Co Const Bdy
Pennine Way
Cairn
Earthwork
Russell's Cairn 619
Split the Deil 610
Pennine Way
Cairn
Windy Gyle
Ford
Sheepfold
Sheepfold
Richard's Cleugh
509
Sheepfold
Routin Well (Spring)
600
590
570
550
Black Braes
Cross Cleugh
Carlcroft Hope
Rough Knowe 462 450
430
Sheepfold
Sheepfold
Sheepfold
Outer Green Cleugh
350
410
440
.457
Swineside Law
The Street
Inner Green Cleugh
Loft Cleugh
Sheepfold
Trows Law
Loft Hill
Sheepfold
Gowkhope Shank
Sheepfold
Ford
Bailey's Cleugh
Sheepfold
Ford
Trows
Sheepfold
Fords
Sheepfold
Stob Cleugh
Stob Hill
FB
286
Shorthope Hill 421
The Slime
FB
Rowhope
Fords FB
Hindside Knowe
Sheepfold
Sheepfold
Stell
Stogie's Cleugh
Cattle Grid 298
Sheepfold
Cattle Grid Ford
Carshope FB
Whar Moor
383
START

In late summer and early autumn, the steep hillside to the right takes on a mottled hue. The dark-green patches are bracken; in September and October when frost arrives, the dying fronds assume many shades of yellow and brown, bringing changing colour to the landscape.

Continue on keeping the fence on your right. Go over the stile at the gated fence ahead and stay on the track as it skirts Swineside Law.

To the left of the track the hillside has been eroded by sheep rubbing hard against the exposed surface to relieve itches or to gain shelter from the weather. Sheep rubs are a convenient way of looking at soil profiles. The section shows a very thin covering of poor humus which is the dark band at the top. Below that is a broader band of leached soil where rainwater has washed out all soluble material. At the bottom, overlying the bedrock is a layer of clay and small stones. A combination of high altitude and heavy rainfall here has produced conditions where few plants can survive successfully; the exceptions include moor mat-grass and heath bedstraw.

Follow the track as it climbs steeply up Black Braes.

This is a good stretch to look for the presence of the large black dor beetles. These creatures are very common in summer on the tracks. They collect dung, bury it, lay an egg in it and then the larvae eat it after they have hatched out. The beetles themselves are a source of food for foxes and kestrels. You may see a fox dropping on the track containing shiny black and blue remains of dor beetles.

Continue on. At the corner of the fence leave The Street and branch right, signed Windy Gyle, to follow another track across rough ground. After descending, then climbing up steeply, you reach the Border fence. Keeping the fence on your left walk on towards Windy Gyle.

Over to the left is Scotland and the valley of the Calroust Burn. Further left still, in the far distance are the Eildon Hills, which the Romans called Trimontium (the three hills); they overlook the border town of Melrose.

Continue along the ridge, past the hollowed-out remains of a stone cairn, to begin the final climb to the summit of Windy Gyle. Cross the stile over the fence next to the gate. Towards the top, the path

bears away left from the fence to reach the large stone mound of Russell's Cairn.

At 619m (2043 feet) Windy Gyle must be one of the most spectacular viewpoints on the Border. To the north lie the fertile valleys of the Scottish lowlands and to the north east the familiar long whaleback outline of The Cheviot. The cairn itself derives its name from Lord Francis Russell, son-in-law of Sir John Forster, Warden of the English Middle March who was responsible for the defence of the central sector of the Border in the reign of Elizabeth I. Lord Russell was reputedly killed at this spot when trouble broke out at a meeting to settle grievances between the English and the Scots on July 27th 1585.

Kelsocleugh and Bowmont Water from Windy Gyle

Leave the cairn by turning right on the route signed to Rowhope and walk towards the gate in the fence.

Wild fruits are rare at this altitude but one to look out for between the cairn and the gate is cloudberry, aptly named because it usually grows above 545m (1800 feet) – in the clouds! It is sometimes known as mountain raspberry but the hill shepherds still refer to it by its Saxon name 'noop'. The plant grows to a height of about 15cm; the broad, five-lobed leaves cradle single white flowers in May or June. In August the berries are a deep orange-red colour.

Cross the stile by the gate and continue straight on downhill, bearing left onto a well-defined path.

Peat has been dug from the hillside left of the path. Until relatively recently farming families in these isolated valleys, far removed from ready supplies of coal, used peats for heating and cooking. The 'dubs' (cuttings), were opened up in May. First the turf sods were removed, then a winged spade was used to cut square or flat peats, which were taken on a peat sledge to less boggy ground and spread out to dry. In good weather, this took 3 to 4 weeks. The peats were then led in by horse and cart, stacked against a wall and protected from the rain by a top layer of 'rashies' (rushes). On average one cartload only lasted one week! The shepherd from Rowhope still comes up to this part of the hill to cut peats.

As the gradient eases at the bottom of the hill bear right to follow the broad green track along the grassy ridge, keeping the wooded valley of the Wardlaw Burn on the far left. Head towards the end of the ridge then on downhill with the Trows Burn on the right. Cross the stile by the gate and continue down the track. Cross the footbridge over the burn and walk on to Trows Farm to join the metalled road.

At Trows, the overhanging eaves on the modern farmhouse up to the right, provide an ideal nesting location for up to 6 pairs of house martins. With a liberal supply of mud about in the farmyard for nest material and no natural cliffs or other houses in the neighbourhood, it's no coincidence that they return here every year to breed.

Once past the buildings, go through the gate, on down the road, past Rowhope Farm and back to Slyme Foot.

Peat cut and stacked in the Coquet Valley

The Rowhope Burn is a favourite haunt of the dipper. Between 1990 and 1992, the National Park organised a Voluntary Warden project to monitor the population of this familiar upland bird. About 25 pairs were located in the upper reaches of the Coquet and its tributaries. Each pair of dippers has a range of about 1.5km, nesting among craggy outcrops or on suitable ledges under bridges. Nests are always built over running water so that the droppings of the youngsters fall directly into the burn and don't betray their presence to predators. Dippers are one of the few birds that stay on in the hill country despite adverse weather conditions. Only when the burns freeze over completely are they forced downstream to open water.

The Cheviot from Windy Gyle

Up, Down and Around

13 Wedder Leap – Fairhaugh – The Middle – Barrow Law.
8km (5 miles); ascent 230m (755 feet); about 3 hours

A short classic walk in the Cheviot foothills with lovely views and without a lot of effort. There are two steep climbs, one long up the flanks of Kyloe Shin and one short through a forest ride near Fairhaugh. There are good tracks most of the way, route finding is easy and the surprise panorama on the final descent makes this walk especially worthwhile.

To reach the start leave the B6341 Rothbury to Elsdon road at Swindon if you are approaching from Elsdon, or at Flotterton, from Rothbury. Both junctions are signed Alwinton. Follow the road through Harbottle to Alwinton. Go through Alwinton and continue on the narrow single track road up the Coquet Valley for about 10km (6 miles). Park in Wedder Leap car park in the trees on the left (GR 866103).
There used to be a school here. It was a prefabricated building, put up in the 1960s to replace the old Victorian school across the river and close to the route of this walk. But numbers dwindled because families moved out of the valley as outbye farms became less viable. The school closed in 1978, since when children have had to travel daily down the valley to the nearest school at Harbottle.

By 1992 the building had become derelict and was an eyesore. The National Park entered into a partnership scheme with the landowner, the Ministry of Defence to tidy up the site. The school was demolished and a car park and picnic area provided for visitors to the valley.

Many of the trees and plants around the site were established by a caring school caretaker. He appreciated their educational potential and their value in providing shelter and a pleasant outlook. County Council ground staff planted the shelterbelt; in 1977, school managers (now called governors) and children put in several hardwoods, including the horse chestnut to commemorate the Queen's Silver Jubilee. The wetland area at the top of the site contains yellow iris, water mint, meadowsweet, sneezewort and greater reed mace (bulrush).

Meadowsweet

Leave the car park. Turn left along the road.
Hard to believe that the dilapidated building on the left was once a popular dance hall. Its claim to fame was that it had the best sprung floor in the whole of Northumberland. The hall was provided for the local people by Major Askew from Berwick who rented the shoot at Uswayford (local pronunciation Yoosyford) higher up the valley. At the end of the shoot he always held a Beaters Ball in the old Victorian school until one year when the floorboards gave way under the feet of a particularly energetic couple. After that Major Askew decided to build a proper dance hall.

Askew Hall was opened in 1935 and for many years when the valley folk were more numerous, it was always a great place for social gatherings. Sadly its only use now is for storing hay.

After about 100m turn right and pause on the footbridge over the River Coquet.
Here the river has cut a passage through solid rock, creating a large, deep pool known as Wedder Leap. Tradition has it that the name originated in the far off days of the Border Reivers. A thief with a stolen wedder slung across his shoulders, attempted to escape from his pursuers by leaping the river at this spot. He was unable to secure a foothold on the opposite bank, the weight of the sheep dragged him backwards into the pool and they both drowned.

The rock crevices and river banks support a variety of flowering plants among them the melancholy thistle, so named after the gentle way it nods its head. Early herbalists, more prolific in Northumberland than anywhere, believed that an infusion made of the leaves would cure lovesick lads of their unhappiness. Although it belongs to the thistle family, this species has no spines and is safe to touch.

Cross the two stiles and walk up the edge of the plantation to the top of the field. Go over the stile by the end of the plantation turn left and continue alongside the wall on the left. Cross the next stile and pause near the two buildings on the left.

The stone building is the old Victorian school opened in 1879 and beside it is the wooden schoolhouse. The first headteacher was Mr. Blythe, a one-armed, well-educated gypsy from Kirk Yetholm who arrived in the valley before the school was built and taught the shepherds' children in the stable at Windyhaugh on the far side of the Coquet. Mr. Blythe stayed for many years and was held in great respect by everyone. 'A man he was to all the country dear' commented the historian of Coquetdale, David Dippie Dixon.

After the school closed it was used as a hay barn but recently has been given a new lease of life as a camping barn. It was renovated by the National Park and the MoD Otterburn Training Area and provides a base for schools and youth groups coming into the valley for field studies and outdoor adventure activities.

Continue past the camping barn and join the stony track on the left. Follow the track as it gradually descends into the valley of the Barrow Burn and then climbs steeply out again. At the top of the hill the track levels out and the view opens up.

To the left is the broad ridge of Barrow Law which is on the return route; beyond Barrow Law, in the far distance lies the long, distinctive form of Cheviot. Immediately ahead, clothed in conifers is Middle Hill and behind, on the horizon, the border with Scotland. Down to the right is the Usway Burn snaking its way past the old steading at Fairhaugh, almost hidden from view by the trees.

Fairhaugh is mentioned in monastic documents dating to 1245. It was one of the summer grazing grounds held by the white-robed Cistercian monks of Newminster Abbey which stood near the county town of Morpeth.

The Camping Barn at Barrowburn during restoration >

For over 300 years they held about 6880 hectares (17,000 acres) of land in Upper Coquetdale where they grazed large numbers of sheep whose wool provided income to maintain the Abbey.

The boarded-up shepherd's house at Fairhaugh was last occupied about 1960 when the Forestry Commission acquired the lease and planted trees on the land.

Continue to the gate across the track. Cross the ladder stile by the gate into the forest.

The conifers on either side of the track are Sitka spruce, a fast-growing tree native to Alaska in North America that produces high quality soft-wood timber very quickly. The Forestry Commission, set up after the First World War to provide timber for industry, opted for Sitka after seeing its success rate in a pioneering project to plant shelter belts on the Duke of Buccleugh's estate in southern Scotland. Sitka's white long-fibred wood is ideal for paper pulp and chipboard. It was a major material used in the construction of the Mosquito aircraft, a high performance light bomber in service during the Second World War.

Keep straight on downhill.

On the edge of the track, most notably on the right, are large tussocks of tufted hair-grass. The key to its identification in ungrazed areas like this, is the plumey flower stem which is often over 1m in height and its coarse, blade-like leaves. Although tufted hair-grass grows in wet places, the tussocks themselves provide a warm, dry environment for invertebrates to hide during the winter. If you shake a tussock, dozens of creatures, particularly in the larval stage, are likely to fall out.

At the hairpin bend near the bottom of the hill, turn left onto a green track which soon begins to climb up a forest ride.

In late summer forest rides provide sheltered feeding areas for dragonflies. The one you are most likely to see is the common hawker. The male is blue and black banded, the female, which is larger, is yellow and brown. Their hunting technique is similar to that of a bird of prey, hence the name hawker. They fly steadily to begin with, looking for insects, then suddenly they jink off to one side seizing their prey with their mandibles and feet and devouring it on the wing.

At the top of the ride bear right onto a track which comes in from the left. Go downhill

and over the stile by the gate across the track. About 50m beyond the forest, bear right onto a narrow path which contours around the hill to the left.

Flowing along the valley bottom to the right is the Usway Burn, one the loveliest tributaries of the River Coquet. The source of the burn is in the peat mosses on the flank of Cheviot; the clear, peaty waters have a 12km journey to make through narrow steep-sided valleys before they join the Coquet at Shillmoor near Alwinton. The track coming down the far hillside above the Usway Burn is Clennell Street, an old drove road, now a linear bridleway route (see Walk 14). The cluster of buildings at the head of the valley is Uswayford, reputedly the most isolated farm in Northumberland.

Uswayford Farm about 1920. Note the haystacks

The path eventually comes to a gate and stile. Cross the stile and with the fence on your right, go towards the fingerpost seen ahead.

The short grass makes for easy walking. It is kept in trim by grazing sheep which prefer the fescues, the sweeter grasses that grow here, rather than the coarser, less palatable moor and mat-grass on the hillsides. Their droppings fertilize the ground, this encourages more growth and so more food for them.

Just before you reach the fingerpost bear left downhill on a sunken track to the Barrow Burn. Cross the burn, go through the wicket gate and uphill on the track to the plantation on the left. Keep straight on to join the forest access road. Follow this to the end of the plantation then turn immediately left to a gate and stile.

The steep ravine on the left is called Murder Cleugh. The origin of the name is unknown; perhaps it was merely an appropriate description for a particularly difficult piece of countryside which shepherds had to negotiate when they looked for their sheep.

Cross the stile. After about 15m turn right onto a grassy track. Carry on along the ridge. After 1.5km pass between two large boulders on the line of an old enclosure wall and continue to Barrow Law; for a spectacular view down the Coquet Valley.

To the left is the imposing summit of Shillhope Law 501m (1644 feet), on the right, Tindale Law, Partridge Side with Dumbhope Law beyond and in the valley bottom the farms of Barrowburn (below) and Windyhaugh on the far bank of the Coquet.

Follow the track downhill and through the gate into the hayfield. Keep to the path.

The hay meadows at Barrowburn Farm provide winter fodder for the sheep. The land is traditionally managed to safeguard the many species of wild flowers that grow there. These include wood cranesbill, ox-eye daisy, red clover and pignut, food plant of the small black chimney sweeper moth.

A walling programme, grant-aided by the National Park is in progress around these inbye fields. Skilled wallers from Harbottle are rebuilding walls that have fallen into disrepair providing shelter for stock and a habitat for spiders, insects and other wild creatures.

Just before you reach the farm buildings turn sharp right along the track. Go through the gate at the end of the track, turn left onto the road.

The two ash trees on the hillside above Windyhaugh Farm on the right are known as 'The Preaching Trees'. In 1903 when David Dippie Dixon was in the area, he noted there were 'three venerable ashtrees'. Apparently Presbyterian ministers from Harbottle held

Windyhaugh Farm

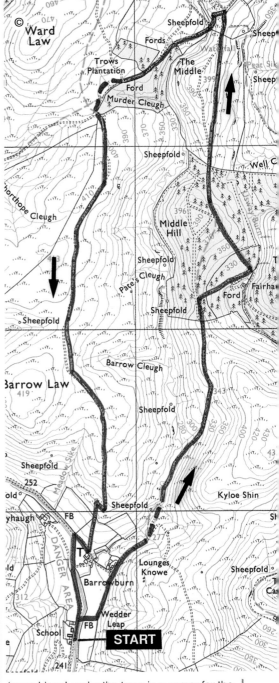

'preachings' under the trees in summer for the local shepherds and their families and even 'people from the Scotch side' came great distances to the meetings.

Follow the Coquet back to the car park.

14

Alwinton – Clennell Street – Copper Snout – Pass Peth.
13 km (8½ miles); ascent 250m (820 feet); about 4½ – 5 hours.

In 1181 Odinel de Umfraville Lord of Redesdale leased the grazing in his forest around Alwinton to the monks of Newminster Abbey near Morpeth. Fourteen years later his grandson Richard gave the monks Kidland.

Odinel's forested glades have long since vanished but the bare-topped hills roamed by medieval monks with their flocks and herds are tramped today by shepherds and walkers. This is a strenuous walk over the monks' old grazing grounds with a long ascent up Clennell Street to begin with, a stiff climb up Pass Peth near the end and a little road walking to finish. Wonderful views, and apart from one or two boggy areas around gates, firm underfoot.

To reach the start, leave the B6341 Rothbury to Elsdon road at Swindon if you are approaching from Elsdon, or Flotterton, from Rothbury. Both junctions are signed Alwinton. Follow the road through Harbottle and continue to Alwinton the last hamlet in Upper Coquetdale. Park in the National Park car park (GR 919063). Turn left at the exit and walk back along the road to the T-junction.

The public house on the right is aptly named The Rose and Thistle, the national emblems of England and Scotland. For several centuries after war broke out between the two nations in 1296, Alwinton situated as it is so close to the Border, suffered from the depredations of fighting men. Today, military personnel still pass through the village but don't leave a trail of havoc and destruction in their wake. On the left, the stone buildings with the big green

doors are pounds or barns. Not long ago sacks of flour, groceries and animal foodstuffs were left here by carriers and suppliers from Rothbury and beyond, to be collected by shepherds living in isolated places further up the valley.

Cross the village green and the footbridge. Turn left onto the road signed Clennell Street/Border Ridge.

Clennell Street is one of many trackways in the border hills frequented in times past by cattle drovers, shepherds, pedlars and whisky smugglers and now a favourite route for walkers. It runs for 19 km (12½ miles) from Alwinton to Cocklawfoot at the head of the Bowmont Water in Scotland.

The name Clennell means 'clean hills' bare of natural woodland; this is the only tree-lined section of the walk, mainly ash, Scots pine and horse chestnut. The young trees in the guards on the right were planted by the National Park in association with the landowner. On the left, the overgrown areas beneath the trees provide a haven for one of Britain's smallest birds, the wren. Resident here throughout the year, it flits about among the vegetation and around the walls seeking out its favourite food, spiders!

Keep on past two farm entrances and carry on uphill on the unmade track.

Hawthorn blossom

To the left and right of the track are a few windblasted hawthorns and dog rose, frail survivors of a once attractive stock-proof hedge. These elderly specimens still manage to produce blossom in summer and berries in autumn. Over the centuries, country folk have gathered this rich harvest from the hedgerows, dark red haws for jelly to spread on scones and bread and cherry red hips to make soothing syrup. Hips had another less beneficial use. Mischievous children would slit open the berries and drop the seeds down peoples' backs, a prank guaranteed to provide endless amusement because the seeds are hairy and irritate the skin so the unfortunate victim has to scratch repeatedly to remove the itch!

Go past the gate and stile on the right. Continue uphill and after crossing the ladder stile by the gate over the track, stop to draw breath and look back to Alwinton in the valley below.

The large field between the village and the river is the site of the Border Shepherds' Show. It is always held on the second Saturday in October and is the last show of the year in the border valleys. The show started in 1874 when local shepherds met together in amiable rivalry with the pick of their flock to see who had the best sheep. Not to be outdone, the womenfolk later decided to hold their own competition for baking. The object of the show was, and still is, to encourage good stock husbandry and to show off various culinary skills through friendly competition. Since then the show has expanded to include dog trialing, horticulture, crafts, exhibitions, trade stands, wrestling, sideshows and amusements and now attracts hundreds of visitors from all over the county.

Carry on up the track past Castle Hills on the left.

Alwinton Show

The small shelterbelt just uphill from Clennell Street cottage on the right is another National Park promoted tree planting scheme for both shelter and appearance. The trees are primarily deciduous species – oak, ash, rowan and hazel.

Go past the entrance to Clennell Street Cottage and continue uphill.

On Camp Knowe the hillside opposite, to the left of the conifer plantation, are the ramparts and ditches of a prehistoric hillfort. It occupies a strong position overlooking the River Alwin below and its confluence with the Coquet further down the valley. The earthwork is one of a number of prehistoric settlements in the area. The fact that several are situated close to Clennell Street would seem to indicate that the drovers road is much older than written records. In medieval documents it is called the

Coquet Valley near Alwinton

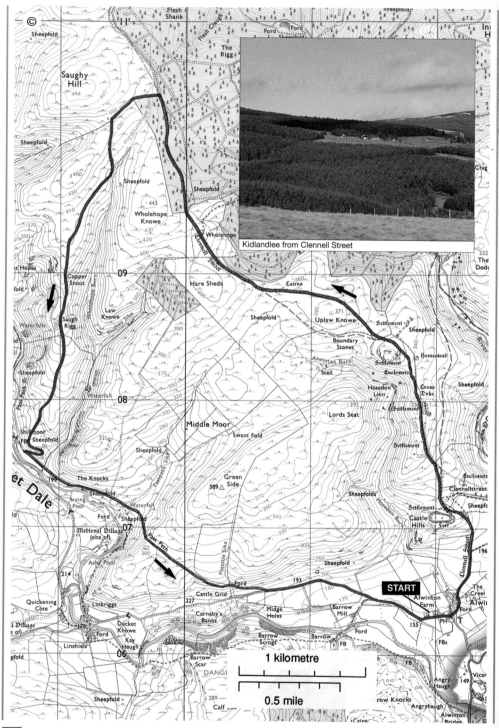

Kidlandlee from Clennell Street

START

74

magnam viam de Yarnspath (the great road of Yarnspath). In all probability Clennell Street does date back to prehistoric times and over the centuries has been used as a major communication and trading route.

A little further on the track dips and passes through a gap in a steep-sided bank about 1m high.

The bank is a cross ridge dyke. Its purpose was to funnel the driven cattle through the gap in a compact group along the drove road, to reduce the chances of them straying down the steeper sides of the ridge.

Follow the track over the next rise.

The settlement in the forest clearing ahead and slightly right, is Kidlandlee. The trees were planted after the Second World War; before then, Kidlandlee stood in splendid isolation on the bare hilltop. The original house was reputedly the result of a bet in a London club to build the highest shooting box in England. The challenge was accepted by Major Leyland who had bought the Kidland estate from the Lambtons of County Durham around 1890. Accordingly in 1904 a shooting box and stables were constructed beside the existing shepherd's cottage and outbuildings at 384m (1260 feet) above sea level.

The estate eventually passed to the Forestry Commission and the house which was more like a mansion than a shooting box, was pulled down by a local builder in the 1950s. The rest of the property has been converted and despite the encroachment of the forest has one of the finest views in the county.

Continue downhill. Cross the stile next to the gate, then a boggy area and bear right. The track passes close by some cairns on the right which are probably prehistoric burials rather than field clearance. It then bears left round a low hill, goes through the next gate and skirts the edge of the conifer wood to reach another gate. Cross the stile by the gate and go up the slope to the ruined building on the right.

This is Wholehope. It used to be a herd's house and was built sometime after the union of England and Scotland in 1603. Although relative peace between the two countries made it possible to resettle the Kidland area, abandoned due to raids by Scots and marauding thieves, old fears died hard. Wholehope together with other new houses at Kidlandlee and Milkhope was built on a hilltop

as before 1603 people living in the bottom of the Alwin Valley had not been able to hear the alarm raised by neighbours in the next valley when there was a raid, because of the high hills between. Wholehope was last occupied in 1942. It then became a Youth Hostel but was closed in 1960 as it was too far away from civilisation to be properly managed.

Go over the stile next to the gate ahead, keep on along Clennell Street and through another gate into the plantation. Continue straight on at the junction of the tracks.

Conifer plantations are usually cool places and the damp grass verge on either side of the forest track is a good habitat for one animal that is often ignored, the slug. The ubiquitous big black slug sometimes comes in attractive orange and brown forms. Slugs feed on rotting vegetation and fungi and will even use their large muscular foot to climb trees to graze on lichens growing on the bark.

Slugs are closely related to snails but as they haven't a shell they don't need to live where there is lime to make the shell. However like snails slugs, far back in their evolution once lived in water. They still have a wet skin so dry conditions are the greatest threat to their survival. For this reason they are more active early morning and evening or through the day in cool, damp weather, especially in spring and autumn. They also hide in dark places or stay still or move slowly to avoid drying out. But their slowness, size and soft body makes them vulnerable to predators such as birds and hedgehogs; their only protection is the sticky mucus (slime) that coats their skin. A thrush will often wipe a slug along the ground to remove the slime before swallowing its prey.

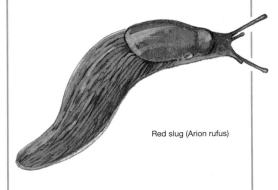

Red slug (*Arion rufus*)

The River Coquet with Shillmoor Farm in the distance

At the end of the plantation go through the gate and after about 150m turn left to leave Clennell Street at the waymarker. Passing the forest on your left, follow the fenceline till you come to a stell on the right.

From here the view looks straight ahead over Kyloe Shin to the Border Ridge on the skyline. To the right is Mozie Law, on its left the long hill is Beefstand, where in a natural bowl, reivers were reputed to conceal cattle before running them across the Border. Left again is Lamb Hill. The Pennine Way which follows the Border Ridge is routed across these three hills.

Cross the stile next to the gate in the fence on the left. Follow the path straight ahead then bear right over the low hill and descend to a stony track. Turn right on to the track; the valley of the Wholehope Burn is on the left and the Usway Burn on the right. Continue along the ridge for about 2km crossing another stile before dropping down towards Shillmoor and the River Coquet.

The narrowest part of the ridge is known as Copper Snout. The name is probably derived from the green colour found in the rock, fragments of which can be seen on the track. Green was only one of a wide range of pastel colours produced in andesite when it was first laid down as volcanic lava about 300 million years ago.

Shillmoor stands at the confluence of the Usway Burn and the River Coquet. In the early 13th century it belonged to Thomas Clennell of Clennell near Alwinton, who granted the flocks and herds of the monks of Newminster, right of passage through his lands to their summer pasture on the hills. Shillmoor now belongs to the Ministry of Defence but its picturesque situation close to the river with the backdrop of hills makes it a popular subject for photographers.

At the bottom of the hill the track meets a wall. Turn sharp left at the fingerpost signed Alwinton and with the wall on your right follow the path to cross the stile ahead and then the Wholehope Burn. Continue around the foot of The Knocks.

The path is Pass Peth, another of the well-documented old drove roads and trackways that criss-crossed the border hills. From its vantage point high above the Coquet the path offers one of the best views down river. On this quiet stretch you may well see a heron, either flying overhead or fishing in the shallows. Herons spend a long time preening. They produce a special 'powder down' on their breasts which is used like talcum powder to soak up slime from eels and other fish but one of their favourite foods is baby rabbits!

After crossing twin tracks and the Pass Peth Sike go through the gate ahead. Bear slightly left, uphill to begin with then diagonally right up the steeply ascending grassy track towards the nick in the top of the hill.

As you climb up Pass Peth look down to the right to the haugh on the far side of the Coquet where you can see the rectangular outlines of a number of buildings. This is the site of the medieval village of Linbriggs. Grass-covered wall footings show there were at least 15 buildings in the village and a corn drying kiln dug into the bankside above the river. A mill is also mentioned in early records.

In the late 16th century detailed accounts were kept of cross-border raids. One entry in the English version, the Calendar of Border Papers, mentions a complaint made by the 'the towne of Allenton (Alwinton) and Linbriggs' against the Elliots, Crosiers and Armstrongs of Teviotdale and Liddesdale 'and 200 others for reiving (stealing) 100 kye (cows) and oxen, 20 horses and meares (mares), spoiling the towne

and taking 20 men prisoners.

The nick at the top of the hill is where the men of Upper Coquetdale kept watch in shifts, day and night to give warning of Scottish raids. Border Laws stated that the day watch of 'Cookdaill' had to begin at Passpeth; 'Allenton to watch Paspethe with two Men every Day'. Anyone not found at his post by the Setters and Searchers of the Watch – local gentry – was liable to a hefty fine.

Continue on over wet ground following the waymarkers to cross the stile in the corner of the field.

The rock face on the far side of the valley is Barrow Scar exposed over the centuries by the action of the River Coquet as it cut down through its bed. The Scar is a record of geological changes over millions of years when, from time to time, the area was covered by shallow seas. The seas deposited alternate layers of mud, sand and shellfish debris which ultimately solidified into shale, sandstone and limestone.

Follow the path alongside the fence to your left and carry on downhill. Cross a stile and a sike and continue to the wicket gate at the bottom of the hill. Go through the gate onto the road and turn left for Alwinton.

View down River Coquet from Pass Peth

15

Holystone Burn Valley – Holystone – Sharperton
7.5 kms (5 miles); ascent 60m (197 feet) about 2 – 2½ hours

Starting from the Forest Enterprise picnic site near Holystone this walk can be done in one attempt or in two. The first leg incorporates part of the Holystone Burn Nature Reserve with its juniper scrub and heather moor. The second part is through Holystone Village, over fields to Sharperton and back by the banks of the River Coquet. It's an easy family walk over firm ground.

Take the road through Holystone village signed Campville and park at the Forest Enterprise picnic site (GR 951026).

PART I: HOLYSTONE BURN VALLEY
Leave the picnic site and turn right onto the tarmac road.

On the left is an old raised field boundary built of earth, faced with stone and colonised or planted with oak and hazel. According to an old saying, it takes an oak one hundred years to grow, one hundred years to stand and one hundred years to die. A family particularly associated with oak trees are the gall wasps. They lay their eggs in the tissues of buds, flowers or leaves.

The tree reacts to the chemicals around the eggs by producing a growth (a gall) around each one to isolate it. This is an example of very sophisticated chemical engineering on

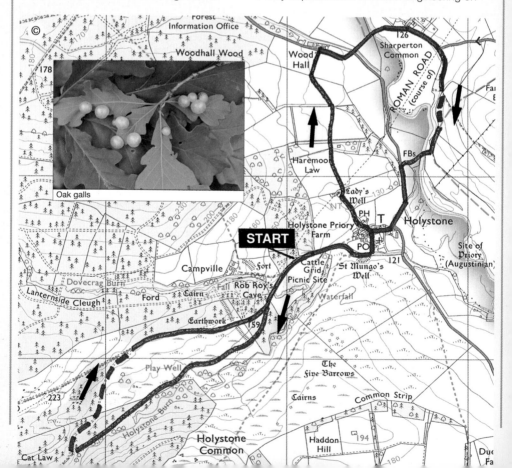

Oak galls

The Holystone Burn Nature Reserve

behalf of the insect. Several different kinds of gall are usually found on oak; oak apples, green and spongy, and marble galls are the most obvious. The undersides of leaves however are often studded with two or three different kinds of spangle gall.

Carry on along the road until you reach the corner of a conifer plantation on the left. Continue for a few metres and look for a step stile over the fence. Cross the stile and follow the cleared path through the trees to the fence on the far side.

The conifers in this plantation are mainly Scots pine and Douglas fir. The Douglas fir is identified by its long brown buds, soft needles and papery scales. It was introduced to Britain from British Columbia in 1827 by the Scottish botanist David Douglas. It grows up to 91m (300 feet) in its native land. In Britain it can reach about 55m (180 feet) which is still a good height. Douglas fir produces excellent timber for telegraph poles, flooring and furniture.

Leave the plantation by the step stile over the fence. Go straight on, keeping to the path across the heather moorland.

This is the Holystone Burn Nature Reserve, owned by Forest Enterprise and managed jointly with the Northumberland Wildlife Trust. The reserve was created largely because of the fine sweep of heather left ungrazed since the Forestry acquired the land and the semi-natural woodland alongside the burn.

As you walk along look for low-growing delicate gorse bushes, no higher than the heather. This is petty (small) whin, a characteristic plant of ungrazed heather moorland. On the exposed peat to either side of the path, you are likely to find one of the daintiest lichen species, the pixie cup lichen. Lichens don't look very appetizing but they are the main foodplant of a family of moths called footmen. Footmen caterpillars are covered with tufts of hair and look like black loo-brushes!

Continue along the path, keeping the trees on your left.

Cross-leaved heath

Plants in the wetter areas of the reserve include cross-leaved heath and bog myrtle. Bog myrtle is a low-growing shrub, no higher than about waist height. It has tiny red flowers which appear before the leaves. When the stems or leaves are bruised they give off a pungent smell of eucalyptus. Country people believed that this smell kept bugs away, which is why bog myrtle used to be called fleawood. In the south of England, bog myrtle is known as sweet gale – a softer name for a softer landscape. Something else to look for along the way are ants' nests. These are mounds of leaf litter; some have been built near the path and are easy to locate. Each mound may hold as many as one million ants. Ants are a very advanced insect group like other social insects such as bees and wasps. Moreover they have been around for 30 million years compared to the estimated one million for humans. They out-number humans by one million to one and they are about one millionth the size of a human being! The ants here are wood ants and like others all over the world, their way of life is successful because they work together for the benefit of the colony rather than for the individual. It's quite interesting to pause by one of these nest mounds and observe the activities of these busy creatures.

Follow the path, as it bears left into the trees and cross a small burn. Walk on, over another small burn and then a large clearing.

The area you are now walking through was planted with Norway spruce, a non-native conifer. After it was clear-felled a more interesting mix of trees was put in, including oak and juniper. Junipers usually spread by cloning. When old trees collapse their branches re-root and satellites are formed around the dying parent plant. Some junipers reproduce from berries which contain a single hard seed. The berries are green and take a whole year to ripen to dark purple.

Juniper berries

The junipers in the wire guards on the right were planted in 1992 by the Northumberland Wildlife Trust. Cuttings were taken from junipers in the reserve, rooted and grown on elsewhere then brought back here to maintain the indigenous stock. The guards have been put round the trees to protect them from being nibbled by roe deer and rabbits.

Although a number of myths and superstitions are associated with juniper, for instance if you chop down a tree, there will be a death in the family – probably your own! – it does have some useful properties. Oil from the berries was once used to flavour gin and in medicine for the treatment of urinary complaints and piles. Unfortunately there is no evidence to support the old belief that drinking an infusion of juniper would restore one's youth!

Birch will quickly colonise the ground from seed from adjacent trees. The mature trees are sometimes adorned with what looks like birds nests but are in fact 'witches broom'. These strange bundles of twigs are the result of a bacterial infection which stimulates twigs to grow out from particular points, forming tufts. Heather and moor grasses have also come in since the conifers were felled but it will take years for the brash and stumps to rot down.

Follow the path through a strip of birch trees and cross another clear-felled area.

On the left of the clearing old oak trees fringe the Holystone Burn. The oaks are covered with bright green mosses and beard-like lichens, indicating a damp but pollution-free atmos-phere. In winter coal tits and treecreepers pick over the mosses and lichens, searching for hibernating spiders, insects and grubs.

At the end of the clearing the path climbs through woodland to meet a broad forest track. Turn right and continue uphill to the tarmac road.

One of the most numerous plants on the track verges is ribwort plantain. It isn't particularly pretty or striking but it is widespread and the commonest plantain in Britain. Again, earlier generations placed great faith in its ability to heal wounds. Shakespeare refers to this in his play 'Romeo and Juliet'. Romeo, commenting on Benvolio's 'broken (grazed) shin' says "Your plaintain-leaf is excellent for that". Plantain is useful to have on any farm where there's livestock; it provides a valuable source of minerals and vitamins lacking in other forage plants.

View over the Holystone Burn with Simonside in distance

Turn right down the tarmac road.

Looking due south as you walk downhill you can see the unmistakable outline of the Simonside Hills, with Tosson Hill prominent on the skyline. To the left is Coquetdale. The stretch of road from here to the conifer plantation, follows part of a Roman road built 2,000 years ago to link two major routes Dere Street and the Devil's Causeway. Good roads allowed troops to move quickly to quell any rebellion against Roman authority.

Continue down the road and either return to the picnic site or keep straight on towards Holystone village for the second part of the walk.

PART II: HOLYSTONE – SHARPERTON

Leave the picnic site, turn left and follow the tarmac road to Holystone Village.

The road runs close to the Holystone Burn on the right. In April clumps of primroses grow along the banksides. They thrive in the damp, shady conditions under the trees. Their leaves radiate out from a central rosette; each leaf is separate so it catches the maximum amount of sunlight.

Pause by the stone well on the right, just before the road bends left into Holystone Village.

This is St. Mungo's Well. St. Mungo, some-times known as Kentigern, was a 6th century Scottish evangelist. He spent a little time in Cumbria but there is no record of his having visited Northumbria let alone Holystone. The well was built in the early 19th century and, according to popular tradition, was the watering place for Muggers (hawkers). In late autumn they took cartloads of Coquet salmon around the local farms and villages. They used an old hill track to get to Elsdon and Otterburn and on the way stopped at the well; so perhaps St. Mungo's is really 'Muggers' Well.

Carry on up the road.

On the right is the Church of St. Mary the Virgin. Although it was largely rebuilt in the mid-19th century the church dates back to medieval times. In the churchyard, strong iron hoops were put round several graves to protect them from grave robbers. On the left is the walled garden of Priory Farm with two early 18th century dovecotes at the corners. Dovecotes are unusual features in this part of the country; these two have been restored as a result of co-operation between the landowner and the National Park.

At the top of the rise keep straight on.

Holystone is a tiny village and until the late 19th century, most of the houses were thatched. One of the oldest buildings is the 17th century Salmon Inn.

Turn left just before the Salmon Inn and take the signposted track to the Holy Well, in the small copse of trees ahead.

In reality the well is a stone-lined water tank fed by an underground spring which never fails. A rough stone at the east end of the well was reputed to be where the 6th century monk Paulinus knelt to carry out his conversions and from this holy stone, the village got its name.

There are all sorts of tales about the origin of the well. Some say it is a Roman cistern, a watering hole for soldiers and travellers who used the Roman road. Others say it is much older, a holy place for the pagan goddess Mother Earth, hence its other name the Lady's Well; and whether it was St. Paulinus or more probably St. Ninian who carried out mass conversions to Christianity is unlikely to be proven. What does matter is that the place has atmosphere and will continue to attract visitors from all over the world.

Follow the track as it bends right, to the ladder stile by the gate. Cross the stile and continue along the edge of the field.

Flocks of lapwing are a familiar sight in these fields. They look black and white as they fly overhead flapping their wings, but observed on the ground their upper parts actually have a dark green metallic sheen. In spring the male performs a tumbling display flight; his call 'peewit' has become another name for this attractive bird. Lapwings are ground-nesting and lay four speckled eggs in a clump of grass.

Go over the stile in the fence. Cross the next field, then a squeeze stile and a step stile in close succession. Keeping the fence on your left, cross another field and go through another squeeze stile. With the fence on your right carry on up a grassy track. Go through the next squeeze stile by the first of two field gates, then down the farm track to the road and turn right.

Wood Hall Farm is on the other side of the road. All that's left of the original 17th century farm steading is part of the garden wall sandwiched between the two outbuildings opposite.

Continue along the road. Pass the T-junction and pause on the bridge over the River Coquet.

The bridge was built in 1995 to replace the original one erected in 1878. Before then travellers had to use a wide, rather difficult ford immediately to the north. In times of flood when the river, fed by the upland burns, rose rapidly, the valley fords were treacherous and sometimes claimed lives. The line of the old ford can still be seen in low water.

‹ Lady's Well, Holystone

In early spring oystercatchers arrive on the shingle to breed. They are very distinctive with their black and white plumage, orange-red beaks and long pink legs. Their courtship ritual consists of a flight chase accompanied by a high-pitched, piping call. Coquetdale was the first inland breeding ground in Northumberland to be recorded for oystercatchers. They began coming in the 1940s probably because their traditional breeding grounds on the coast were disturbed by visitors. The oystercatchers which breed here are from the west coast.

Keep straight on along the main road passing Sharperton on the left.

Like Holystone, Sharperton too has a long history. It is first mentioned in 1244 when Thomas of Sharperton was one of the jurors at the inquest into the death of Gilbert de Umfraville who held the Lordship of Redesdale. The Potts and the Dodds are two Sharperton families whose names appear frequently in historical documents. Michael Potts for instance, was one of the witnesses against King Charles I at his trial in 1648-49. Other names mentioned in documents relating to Sharperton are Charlton, Hall, Dixon, Redhead, Turnbull and Robinson.

Carry on until the road bends to the left. At the bend go through the wicket gate on the right and, keeping the fence and hedge on your left, follow the path up through the trees. At the next wicket gate, pause and look back up the Coquet.

In the middle distance, just visible in the trees to the left of the river, are the ruins of Harbottle Castle. Here, on October 15th 1511, Henry VIII's sister Margaret gave birth to a daughter afterwards grandmother of James VI of Scotland and I of England. This scrubby area used to be part of Sharperton Common. It hasn't been subject to a lot of grazing, so a variety of wild flowers and shrubs have survived; among them, blackthorn. Blackthorn

Harebells

belongs to the plum family. It has starry white flowers in March and April followed by small, hard green fruits, sloes, which eventually turn black in autumn.

Go through the wicket gate and with the fence on your right, walk downhill to the footbridge across the Coquet.

In summer, the bankside between the fence and the river is ablaze with colour. Wild flowers grow in profusion on the rich, sandy soil – blue harebells, purple betony, creamy meadow-sweet and tall, slender spikes of yellow agrimony. Agrimony has been used as a medicinal herb since the time of the ancient Greeks; Chaucer, the 14th century English poet best known for his Canterbury Tales, recommended the plant for "alle woundes and bad back".

Cross the footbridge.

The footbridge carries the right of way across the Coquet. In the mid-1980s the bridge was in a dangerous condition. Because of its length – sufficient to span the river in flood – repair costs could have proved prohibitive; but grant-aid from the National Park helped the County Council to retain the bridge.

Keep to the track across the field, go over the step stile, turn left and follow the road back to Holystone village.

Of the Benedictine nunnery founded at Holystone in 1124 nothing remains save fragments of medieval masonry built into the walls of Mill Cottage (The Kennels) on the left, the churchyard wall and the nave of the church.

Return to the car park and picnic site.

Oystercatcher

16 The Grasslees Burn – Darden Lough and Darden Pike. 6.5km (4 miles); ascent 254m (833 feet); about 2½ hours

A challenging walk on permissive paths over glorious heather and bracken-covered moorland to visit a remote hilltop lough (lake) and a panoramic viewpoint. Conditions underfoot are good in all but the worst weather. The undulating route is well waymarked so unless visibility is poor, navigation should not be a problem. Please keep to the paths as all the surrounding land is managed as a grouse moor.

Park in the layby 1km north east of Grasslees Farm on the B6341 Rothbury to Elsdon road (GR 959982). Go through the wicket gate by the fingerpost signed Darden Lough and bear diagonally right down the field and across the pasture to the bridge over the Grasslees Burn.

The burn, a tributary of the River Coquet flows through one of the few remaining areas of semi-natural deciduous woodland in the National Park. Alder dominates this stretch of the burn. The alders by the bridge are mature trees though they are not particularly tall; under more favourable conditions they will grow straight and reach heights of around 19m (62 feet).

The bark gets thicker and rougher as the tree ages and if you look closely at the cracks between the scales you may find all kinds of beetles, bugs and spiders living there. They in turn are the food of woodpeckers and tree creepers which probe the cracks with their long, sharply pointed beaks and prehensile tongues to winkle out a juicy morsel.

Cross the bridge then the stile over the fence and follow the track uphill. Near the top the track forks. Go straight ahead keeping the fence on your left.

The route climbs over terraces of fell sandstone deposited about 280 million years ago by the shallow waters of a large river delta. Compacted beds of sand laid down on top of one another are visible in the rock outcrops along the way. Weathering produces the leached acid soil responsible for heather moorland the characteristic vegetation of these high Fell Sandstones.

Continue on. After a short descent step across the burn and make for the edge of the conifer plantation. The path then bears right away from the wood towards a fence which appears on the left.

The rugged crag to the left is Key Heugh which overlooks the wild and rocky ravine of the Darden Burn. The long, dark ridge beyond is Tosson Hill.

Keeping the fence in sight, follow the path as it winds up through the heather for about 1.5km.

As you walk you may notice bare areas of moorland black with the charred stems of heather. This is the result of managed moor burning to remove old heather and encourage the growth of new shoots from seeds that have lain dormant in the damp peat for several years. The fire warms the seeds to 50° – 60°C and this, combined with the moisture helps them germinate. Should uncontrolled heather burning occur in prolonged dry weather the peat itself will burn and destroy the dormant seeds so the heather will decline.

Heather plays a central role in the life of the moor. Many creatures depend on it for food and shelter. Fresh young leaf growth is as important to sheep grazing the moor in winter as it is to the resident red grouse or the caterpillars of the emperor moth; the bright green

Emperor moth

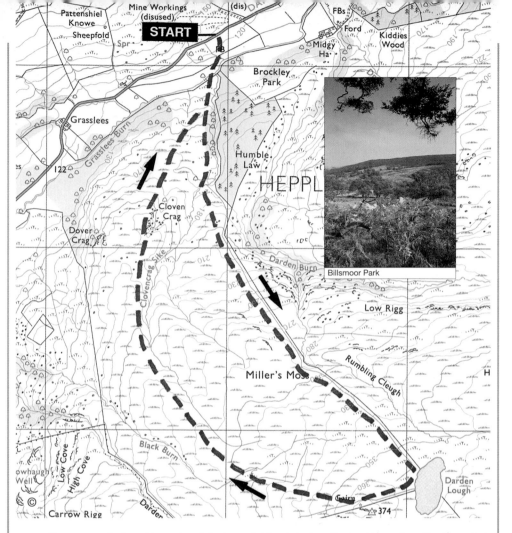

Billsmoor Park

caterpillars are easily found by colour-blind people because to them, they are red, otherwise they are well camouflaged. This is also a good habitat for bees and for spiders which are part of the grouse's diet.

As you crest the last rise Darden Lough comes into view.

The lough lies in a depression carved out of the bedrock by the movement of an ice sheet which covered the north of the country thousands of years ago. When the temperature rose the ice receded and as it did so, meltwater drained into the depression forming a lake.

The peat-stained water attracts little wildlife because it is acidic and very cold, although it is known that leeches were caught here in the early 19th century for doctors who wanted to

bleed their patients. At one time blackheaded gulls used to nest on Darden Lough but with the development of Caistron Nature Reserve a few miles further down the valley, the gulls have all moved off to this more favourable site. There is no cover for nesting birds and whilst you may see a few tufted duck on the water it is unlikely that any will have nested in the area. On the other hand, mallard do nest on the moorland.

Follow the path down to the lough then bear right uphill alongside the fence on your left to the cairn on Darden Pike 374m (1227 feet).

The panorama is impressive. Start by facing the lough and turn in a clockwise direction. On the skyline the treetops of Harwood Forest can be seen rising above the edge of the moor;

moving right, the masts on Ottercops Moss near the A696 come into view. To their right are the waste heaps of Blaxter's stone quarries. In the middle foreground on the valley floor is Elsdon village and behind in the far distance Redesdale Forest.

Carter Fell on the horizon and to its right Thirlmoor at the head of Coquetdale, mark the Border with Scotland. Moving right again along the border line is Windy Gyle, the long back of Cheviot and the conical top of Hedgehope. Between the Border and the Grasslees Valley below lies the Ministry of Defence Otterburn Training Area. To complete the circle the fertile valley of the River Coquet with the red scar of Biddlestone Quarry leads round to Tosson, at 440m (1444 feet) the highest point on the Simonside ridge.

Return to the path, turn left downhill and follow the waymarkers, bearing right and passing above a rock outcrop. Continue across wet ground to a low ridge which gradually bears right for about 1.5km.

It is worth pausing to look at the landscape. The Grasslees Valley has great natural beauty. The bright green pastures cultivated and worked by farming families are richly complimented by the deep colours of the heather and bracken on the hillsides above, especially in late summer and autumn.

The walled and wooded area down to the left is Billsmoor Deer Park. In 1828 the Northumberland historian the Reverend John Hodgson described it as 'a tract of ground, on both sides of Keenshope burn, spread over with brown and heathy knolls, rocky brows, scroggy

Sheep's sorrel

hirsts of hazel and the sloe-thorn, stunted oaks, little birchen shaws, and shapeless waterside clumps of willow and alder, and all wild and brakey, just as a deer-park should be'. There are a few deer in the park but you would have to be here early in the morning or around dusk and bring binoculars to see them.

At the end of the ridge keep on downhill over a rough boulder-strewn area and then bear right along the edge of the valley. Grasslees Farm is down to the left.

Something you will see in the open areas free from bracken is sorrel. Sorrel doesn't grow very tall on these thin acid soils; it doesn't have beautiful flowers but its leaves do have a reddish hue in autumn which adds colour to the moorland. Sorrel is related to dock. Some species are edible and the leaves have a pleasant, slightly acid taste.

Follow the path until you reach the junction with the track. Turn left downhill and retrace your steps to the layby.

Looking north west to Carter Fell from Darden Pike

Cairns, Carvings and Cists

Lordenshaws – Whitton Dene – Whitton Hillhead.
6km (4 miles); ascent 45m (148 feet); 2 – 2½ hours

Ancient settlements, burials and carved rocks feature in this gentle moorland walk across one of the most historic landscapes in the National Park. The beginning and end of the walk are on permissive paths so please keep to the waymarked route except on Lordenshaws hilltop where there is open access around the fort.

A short stretch of the walk is on a single track tarmac road and apart from a shallow burn to cross, there should be no difficulty at all on the route.

To reach the start take the B6342 south of Rothbury for about 3km (2 miles). Turn right on the sharp bend near the National Park boundary sign and continue on the single track road for about ½ mile to the National Park car park at Lordenshaws (GR 053988).

The information panel in the car park explains how Lordenshaws is managed as a grouse moor and as a working hill farm.

Lordenshaws has always been a popular place for visitors who come to walk, picnic and appreciate the heather moorland. In the early years of this century folk journeyed to Rothbury by bus and train from Tyneside and from the mining towns and villages of mid-Northumberland to spend the day on the moors. After the Second World War as cars became affordable, increasing numbers of people came to Lordenshaws, parking on the grass verges and unwittingly destroying the fragile roadside vegetation. The car park was provided for visitors in 1993 as part of a management agreement between the land-owner the Northumberland Estates, the tenant farmer and the National Park.

From the car park side of the road, and with the brooding ridge of Simonside behind you, walk uphill on the left-hand waymarked track. At the next waymarker turn right and continue to the top of the hill.

The summit of Lordenshaws is crowned by a hillfort built 2500 years ago. Whoever built the fort chose the best possible site. It has a tremendous vantage point overlooking the Upper Coquet Valley and is protected from the prevailing wind by the long ridge of Simonside.

Lordenshaws Farm and Simonside

The fort defences consist of three concentric rings of banks and ditches originally topped by a wooden palisade around a small living area no more than 61m across. The houses inside would have been round and also built of timber, plentiful at that time. The main entrance to the fort is on the east and is flanked by two large stones on either side of a sunken track leading downhill.

Why the hillfort had so many impressive defences no-one knows. Was there danger from other humans or from wild animals? Or did the occupants just want to make sure that their cattle and sheep were kept safe at night? Whatever the answer, later settlers also thought this was an ideal place to live. About 100AD they took advantage of the site and built their little settlement of round stone houses inside the fort and even levelled the defences in one area to squeeze in two more.

Walk through the hillfort to the entrance and out by the sunken track. Go downhill to the next waymarker, turn left and head towards the waymarker on the skyline. Continue across an earth bank marking the line of an old field boundary, to a waymarker beside a small but obvious mound in the heather on the left.

This is an ancient burial cairn. It consists of a pile of earth and stones erected over the grave of someone who died in the Bronze Age, more than 3,500 years ago. Of special interest are the exposed rocks decorated with cup marks. At one time these mysterious carvings were thought to be Bronze Age but in fact they are much earlier.

Carry on downhill, following the direction of the waymarkers to a stile in the fence ahead.

On the way look for two exposed Bronze Age cists. These rectangular stone-lined graves were originally each covered by a cairn. The graves are small because the body was buried in a crouched (foetal) position, the idea possibly being to return them to Mother Earth just as they were before birth. In some instances the dead person was cremated and the remains interred in a clay pot.

Cross the stile and walk downhill to another stile.

Ahead, Rothbury, capital of Upper Coquetdale, straddles the valley; further right on the far hillside is Cragside Estate. The rock-strewn land was bought by William Armstrong the famous 19th century Tyneside gunmaker. He began work on the house and grounds in 1863 and, according to D. D. Dixon, the Coquetdale historian, within 21 years he had 'transformed a howling wilderness into a very Garden of Eden'. Cragside was built using local labour and stone quarried on site; it was the first house in England to be lit by electric light. Perhaps Armstrong's greatest achievement and one that gave him most pleasure was the transformation of a barren, rocky hillside to a beautiful wooded estate, with lakes, terraces, alpine gardens and 50km (31 miles) of carriageways.

Following the waymarked path continue downhill to the burn.

On the gentle slope to the right are the grass-covered earthworks of a medieval farmstead with long houses, field walls and yards for cattle. In late spring the hillside is covered with bluebells. Badgers like bluebells, they dig up the bulbs and eat them. They also dig up wasps' nests and bees' nests, but in winter they often make do with earthworms.

The Whitton Burn at the bottom of the hill runs through quite a steep valley in places before it joins the River Coquet to the south east of Rothbury. In the shallow, more open

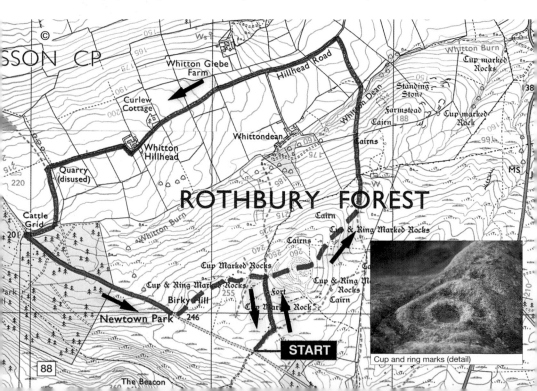

Cup and ring marks (detail)

muddy edges along the burn there are a number of water-loving plants. Water-cress grows in abundance at the crossing place. In pasture land such as this, its hollow stems provide a suitable home for the eggs of the liver fluke, a parasite of sheep and humans, so it is advisable not to eat it.

Water-cress

Cross the burn and walk uphill to the fence ahead. Go over the stile and, keeping another fence on your right continue up the field to the gate. Go through the gate and turn left onto the farm road. Continue on past a turn to the left.

The roadside verge is allowed to grow wild. Two familiar umbrella-shaped plants you should see are cow parsley which flowers in early spring and hogweed, in late June. Hogweed grows up to 2m in height and has large, hairy leaves, cow parsley is much smaller with fern-like leaves.

The flat creamy-white flowers of hogweed act as landing pads for beetles, wasps and hoverflies, all attracted to the nectar and all essential to the business of pollination. In winter the plant remains standing long after the flowers and leaves have gone. The reason lies in the toughness of the ridged stems. Although they also die, the ring of strengthened tissue that surrounded the soft central pith, becomes woody in winter and keeps the plant upright.

Hoverfly

Follow the track uphill, crossing three cattle grids to Whitton Hillhead Farm. Go through the field gate and bear left around the front of the farmhouse. Turn right and continue to the next gate. Go through this gate, turn left through another gate and on along the grassy track keeping the fence on your left. Go through another two field gates, then turn left and follow the fence on your left downhill.

The fence is the march or boundary fence between Great Tosson Farm and Whitton Hillhead. The word march is derived from the French 'marcher' meaning to walk. The term was introduced to this country after the Norman Conquest 1066 when frontiers were established between England and Wales and England and Scotland. A string of heavily garrisoned castles were built in these areas and the Marcher Lords who lived there were responsible for patrolling the Border and keeping the peace. This march fence also marks the boundary of the National Park.

At the bottom of the hill go through the wicket gate into the plantation. Turn right, walk through the wood to another wicket gate. Go through and turn left onto the tarmac road. Follow the road as it passes between the trees and uphill to the open countryside. At the top of the hill turn left at the waymarker and follow the grassy track across Birky Hill.

About 5m to the left of the third waymarker is the Horseshoe Rock, so called because the horseshoe-shaped motif is unusual. Most prehistoric rock art takes the form of shallow cups surrounded by concentric rings cut into the surface of the sandstone boulders and outcrops.

The significance of these carvings is unknown. Historians and archaeologists have all sorts of theories from crude maps to artistic representations of prehistoric settlements. Similar motifs are found elsewhere in Britain, often in association with grave mounds – notably in Ireland and Scotland – and usually on the sandstones which are easiest to carve. Since the people who made these marks have left no evidence of their meaning, prehistoric rock art is likely to remain an unsolved mystery.

Return to the path and continue uphill to the junction of paths and the waymarker passed on the outward journey. At the waymarker turn right and walk back to the car park.

18 Lordenshaws – Spylaw – Coquet Cairn – Simonside.
10km (6½ miles); ascent 220m (673 feet); about 4½ hours

A splendid walk across some of the loveliest heather moorland in the National Park and ending with superlative views of Coquetdale from the lofty heights of Simonside. Whatever time of year you tackle this walk choose a clear day to fully appreciate the vast panorama spread out before you.

The going is not too arduous but on the final leg there is a steep scramble from the forest road to the top of Simonside. Part of the walk is over a grouse moor so please keep strictly to the waymarked route. There are good paths and tracks most of the way, however one longish section across a mire (peat bog) is wet in all but the driest weather.

To reach the start take the B6342 south of Rothbury for about 3km (2 miles). Turn right on the sharp bend near the National Park boundary sign and continue on the single track road for about ½ mile to the National Park car park at Lordenshaws (GR 053988).
The land on both sides of the road is owned by the Northumberland Estates. In July 1992 a Management Agreement was signed between the landowner, the tenant farmer and the National Park to conserve the quality and character of the moorland and to improve public access to the wealth of archaeological remains especially those on the north side of the road (see Walk 17).

One of the main concerns was the damage caused to the heather moor and to the archaeological sites by over-wintering of cattle in the area. Persistent trampling at feeding stations and favourite sheltering places was destroying the vegetation which was unable to recover in the winter. As part of the Management Agreement the cattle now spend the winter in sheds at Holling Hill Home Farm.

Leave the car park in the direction indicated by the fingerposts to Spylaw and Coquet Cairn. Follow the path up the side of The Beacon to the first waymarker beside an obvious heather-covered bank.

The bank which bends away right, up the hillside, is what is left of a medieval deer park wall. The deer park lay within the Forest of Rothbury. For years it was a bone of contention between the commoners who had grazing rights in the forest and Robert Fitz Roger who held the land. In 1275 he enclosed part of the forest for his deer park, blocking off traditional grazing routes. Rumour had it that he gave 6 acres of land to the local parson to prevent him objecting. The commoners were so angry that they took Robert to court. There is no record of the outcome but interestingly old trackways breach the park wall in many places.

The Beacon is so called because in the troublesome times of the 16th century the hilltop was where the men of Coquetdale kept nightly watch 'to give warning to all the holl country of the invasions of the Scottes in England.'

At the waymarker take the left-hand path up and over the hill and down to the sleeper bridge across the Grain Sike burn. Continue on the clear track around the hill to a gate in the fence ahead.

The area you are crossing is a typical upland grouse moor. The underlying fell sandstone rock is very acid and produces a peaty soil that suits heather. Red grouse need young heather for food and long heather for nesting.

Heather

Management of the moor is aimed at providing the right conditions for these game birds; it requires the gamekeeper to burn patches of heather in rotation about every 8 to 10 years. This is why on well-managed moorland you will see patches of older heather mixed with younger and newly-burnt heather.

Do not go through the gate but turn right and, keeping the fence on your left continue to the gate across the track. Go over the ladder stile by the gate and follow the track, turning left in front of the wood. With the wood on your right continue round to the front of Spylaw.

The house has long been deserted and even scout groups who occasionally used it in recent years seem to have abandoned it. In its lifetime, Spylaw was a typical old Northumbrian farmhouse with the living rooms at one end and the byre and henhouse at the other. All the windows apart from one, face south to gain the maximum amount of sunlight. The shelter wood of Scots pine with occasional beech and Norway spruce gives protection to the north and west. Living in such a remote spot, the occupants must have been almost self sufficient. The garden at the front of the house would have provided most of their vegetables and soft fruit.

Cross the stile over the fence in front of Spylaw and turn right heading past a new plantation to another fence and stile. Go over this stile, on downhill and cross a small burn. Follow the waymarked path over rough ground to the Forest Burn. Cross the plank bridge and go uphill on the track past a fenced enclosure on the right.

The Forest Burn area is important for its conservation and landscape interest. The relict woodland along the burn, mainly alder with

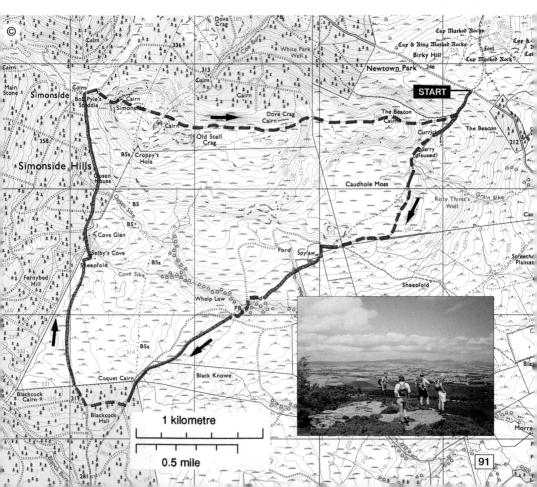

some birch and willow, has gradually declined in the last 40 years because grazing has prevented natural regeneration. The National Park has fenced several areas by the burn to exclude sheep and encourage regeneration. Some oak and ash protected by bio-degradable tubes, have been planted for their additional conservation value.

At the junction of tracks at the top of the hill, take the waymarked path ahead and cross the open heather moorland to a fence on the skyline. Cross the stile in the fence and turn right to follow the path over the hill towards the edge of the forest and Coquet Cairn.

The reason why Coquet Cairn was built in this prominent position is unknown. It could have marked the site of an ancient burial or the 18th century boundary between the estates of the Duke of Northumberland and the Duke of Portland. Boundary stones incised with the initials N or P on opposite faces have been erected at intervals elsewhere on the line of demarcation between the two estates. The vantage point of the cairn gives a wide-ranging view of the countryside. With the forest behind you and looking to the left of the track is the long ridge of Simonside. The summit is at the extreme left, to its right is Old Stell Crag. Right again is Dove Crag and behind Spylaw, The Beacon. To the right of the track the view opens out down the Coquet Valley to the sea in the far distance. Looking further right, the prominent hill with the plantation spilling over the top is Coldrife.

From Coquet Cairn, cross the stile near the corner of the fence and follow the track leading into the forest. The track soon opens out onto a wide ride. Turn right and continue to the forest road. Turn right on the road and almost immediately at the bend, right again along a grassy track to the edge of the forest. Go over the stile next to the gate and follow the waymarked route to the entrance of Selby's Cove, the rocky gorge ahead.

The low-lying land to the right of the path is an area of blanket peat. It began to develop about 3-4000 years ago due to a deterioration in the climate to colder, wetter conditions. The bog moss which grows here holds water and this spongy habitat or mire, is ideal for a number of rare plants. Mires are usually found in the west of the county on the Northumberland/Cumbria border; this one is notable for being so far east.

Cotton grass

Unfortunately land drainage and an increase in the number of sheep in recent years have resulted in the loss of sphagnum moss and the more intimate variety of plants associated with the mire and as a result it is now dominated by cottongrass. Selby's cove is reputedly named after an infamous 17th century robber who had his hideout here. The cove is a fine example of a glacial meltwater channel formed at the end of the last Ice Age about 12,000 years ago. Meltwater from the ice caps covering the Simonside Hills gouged out this deep cleft in the rock strata. Today, most of the natural

View north to the Cheviot Hills from Simonside

drainage occurs on the far side of the Simonside ridge and the cove is now dry.

Follow the waymarked path uphill to the corner of the forest. Cross the stile over the fence and walk downhill through the trees. Cross three sleeper bridges and carry on. The path takes you uphill on a sunken trackway used by drovers and their cattle, along the edge of the forest to meet a forest road. Turn right at the road and take the steep path to the summit of Simonside to begin the long, spectacular ridge walk back to the car park.

The panorama from Simonside is one of the finest views in the whole National Park. To the left, the stretch of water in the foreground is Caistron, a gravel quarry and a nature reserve. Beyond that is the Upper Coquet Valley leading up to the Border Ridge. Moving gradually right are three of the highest border hills, Cheviot with its long whaleback, then Hedgehope then Dunmoor. Further right again are the heather-clad sandstone ridges of Ros Castle and Bewick Moor and a little closer Long Crag, Coe Crag and Cartington Hill. In the near foreground is Rothbury with Cragside Estate behind.

Path to Dove Crag

Follow the path waymarked by Forest Enterprise red arrows. At the junction of paths just past the cairn, keep left and continue to Dove Crag, the next high point on the ridge.

The conifer forest below the crag was planted by the Forestry Commission in the late 1950s – early 1960s. The trees are mainly lodgepole pine, introduced from North America. They can find enough nourishment in the poor, wet soils on these hillsides to survive and they can also withstand exposed positions, but nationally they haven't proved a commercial success.

On the summit of Dove Crag are the remains of a Bronze Age burial cairn, a mere fraction of the rich archaeological heritage of the Lordenshaws area (see Walk 17).

Keep on, following the red waymark arrows then gradually descend the hill to the junction of paths about half way down. Take the right-hand path, continue down to the fence at the bottom and cross the step stile. Go uphill again and along the ridge to the next high point, The Beacon. From here follow the path downhill to the car park.

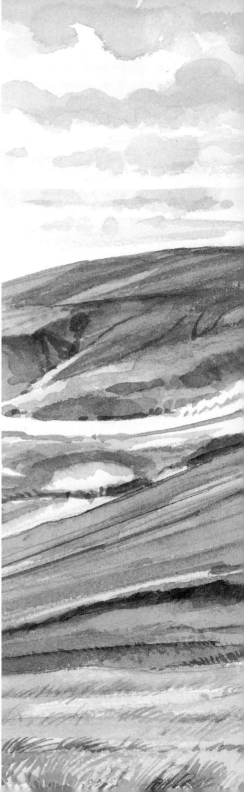

Glossary

Bastle defensible farmhouse. **Haughland** flat land by a river or burn. **Inbye** improved land near the farm buildings. **Lonnen** a green lane. **Outbye** unimproved land furthest away from the farm buildings. **Rake** to roam about. **Scree** hill slope covered with unstable small stones. **Sike** ditch or small burn. **Spate** flood. **Stell** a circular stone enclosure for sheltering sheep. **Wedder** a castrated male lamb.

Further Reading

Upper Coquetdale David Dippie Dixon *1903 (Reprint 1987)*

Comprehensive Guide to Northumberland W. W. Tomlinson *(eleventh edition 1969)*

The Cheviot Way of Life Tony Hopkins *Northumberland National Park 1993*

Notes